Regarding Religious Education

Regarding Religious Education

Mary K. Cove
and
Mary Louise Mueller

Religious Education Press
Mishawaka   Indiana

Library of Congress Cataloging in Publication Data

Cove, Mary K
  Regarding religious education.

  Includes bibliographical references.
  1. Christian education.   I.   Mueller, Mary Louise,
joint author.   II.   Title.
BV1471.2.C67   268   77-10873
ISBN 0-89135-011-X

2 3 4 5 6 7 8 9 10

Religious Education Press, Inc.
Box 364
Mishawaka, Indiana 46544

Material in Chapter II is taken from W. James Popham and Eva I. Baker,
SYSTEMATIC INSTRUCTION, © 1970, p. 17. Reprinted by permission of Prentice-Hall, Inc., Englewood Cliffs, New Jersey.

*Religious Education Press publishes books and educational materials exclusively
in religious education and in areas closely related to religious education. It is
committed to enhancing and professionalizing religious education through the
publication of significant scholarly and popular works.*

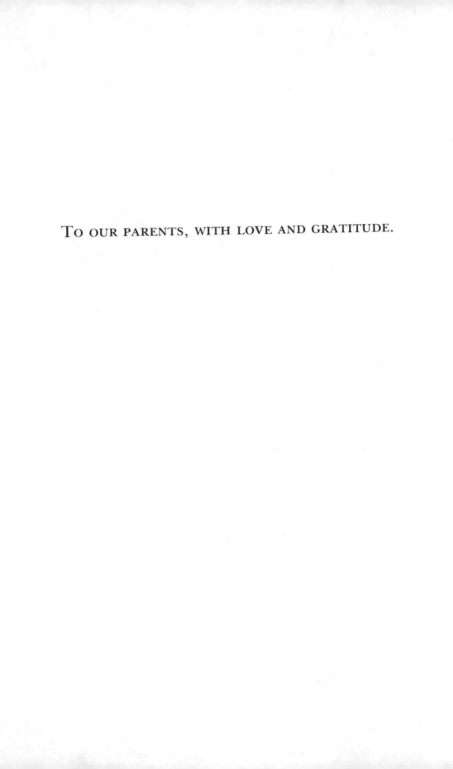

To our parents, with love and gratitude.

Contents

Preface

To all who are engaged in the process of religious education, we invite you to come and read. Each chapter of this book was written with you in mind. It is our hope that from your reading and discussion of the topics presented you will be strengthened in your resolve and encouraged in your efforts to make religious education make a difference. While we would hope you would peruse this work from cover to cover, each chapter can be read as a self-contained treatment of the topic given in the title. Discussion and implementation of the suggestions incorporated in the following pages will sharpen your perspective and in turn improve our religious education efforts. We invite you to write to us: if you agree or disagree, but particularly if you experiment we would like you to share your results.

M. L. MUELLER
San Antonio, TX

M. K. COVE
Springfield, MA

I

Teaching for Living

Religious education through the ages has worn many faces. Even in the years of the twentieth century alone it has appeared among us in differing guises. Teaching for understanding the faith . . . teaching for believing . . . teaching for knowing . . . teaching for being . . . teaching for the practice of religion; each has claimed to be, in varying degrees, what religious education is all about. Today, prophetic religious education is "teaching for living."

The following dialogue attempts to examine "teaching for living" as an aspect of religious education and, in doing this, to integrate it within a general concept of religious education. It is hoped that such a study will prove helpful for what appears in the following chapters. For purposes of clarification, an interested religious educator (RE) dialogues with Anne Burgess (AB), a leader in the current efforts to update religious education in the diocese of Maitland, Australia.

RE: Why do you consider another focus for religious education necessary? Don't you agree that religious education is teaching for understanding . . . for believing . . . for knowing and practicing religion?

AB: Certainly all of these are *part* of religious education. However, too often one or an other of these parts has been picked out as if it were the total religious educa-

3

tion. Simply stated, religious education is education in religion . . . a very broad undertaking.

RE: It seems to me that "education in religion" implies two different notions about religious education. One is a rather academic study of religion, or of any one religion, as a cultural, ritualistic, and ideological phenomenon. The other implies a similar study, but to a lesser extent, within the more general objectives of an education in living religiously. More clearly, these understandings of religious education can be differentiated as an education *about* religion or as an education *in* religion.

AB: I find both equally valid approaches to religious education.

RE: Yes, but they are *different.* Hence the goals and the teaching processes which one chooses to reach these goals would also differ considerably. Take prayer, for example which, in one form or another is an aspect of all religions. It isn't difficult to see that teaching-learning *about* prayer and teaching-learning *to* pray might intersect in some elements but they certainly are not coextensive. So it would seem essential for the congruity of the overall religious education effort that the religious educator makes quite explicit which concept of religious education is being adopted.

AB: What James Michael Lee has summarized in his *The Purpose of Catholic Schooling* seems to have been paralleled in Christian religious education during the twentieth century. The understanding and the practice of religious education have fallen into three main trends. One, the intellectualist approach, equates the purpose of religious education with understanding the faith and knowing about religion. A second trend, which Lee calls moralist, equates religious education with the spiritual formation of students. The third main trend, the integralist, attempts to incorporate the strengths of the two former approaches, and to involve the learner totally in both understanding and experience. These trends are not necessarily chronological. Often all three exist contemporaneously.

RE: Even these three trends seem to fall within the two broad notions of religious education which we mentioned.

AB: Yes, the intellectualist approach to religious education seems based on the notion that religious education is knowing or understanding religion or a religion. Both the moralist and the integralist approaches, with their emphasis upon formation and living, seem based on the notion of religious education as an education in religious living.

RE: It is fairly obvious that your assumption of "teaching for living" as a focus of religious education rests upon the second concept that religious education is an education in religious living. Why do you emphasize this aspect?

AB: Before I answer that, I would want to underscore that I am not opposing knowing and living. On the contrary, religious education as an education in religion, must attempt to integrate all aspects of life, including these two. It is inaccurate, anyway, to separate knowing and living... one can know intellectually, one can know intuitively, and one knows, often with certitude, from the basis of one's experience. One does not stop living while he learns, whether that learning is cognitive, affective, or experiential. Even to separate these ways of knowing and learning is a much easier exercise to perform on paper than in day-to-day existence.

RE: Nevertheless, since around the middle of the twentieth century, educators and educationists seem to have highlighted the separate realms of cognitive and affective.

AB: This is probably best explained as a reaction to the long neglect of the affective aspect in schooling.

RE: Recent work in value education and moral education has recognized this previous narrowing and has pointed to the value of including both elements in formal education.

AB: Again, I am not undermining the intellectual but trying to show the interplay of all activities in a person. It is obvious that understanding is very much a part of our ability to perform motor skills, for example, basketball; social skills, for example, communication; and volitional ones, for example moral decisions. Knowledge helps form attitudes, for example, history gives perspective to present events and contributes to a sense of tradition. It is time for formal education, including formal religious education, to attempt to operate from a notion of student-humanity as an entity. Maslow, Jung, and Erikson, among other psychologists, pose integration as the goal to which human development is directed. If only educators could think of persons as entities and implement their education along this principle!

RE: Since we humans act somewhat according to expectations of us the effects could be astounding! By thinking of man in dualities such as cognitive-affective and body-soul, we really perpetuate self-notions which not only are false but also restrict integration.

AB: But, to return to your original question: Why do I emphasize living as an aspect of religious education? The appropriateness of teaching for living as an integral aspect of religious education rests upon my understanding and experience of religion as a way of life.

RE: Do you mean as a set of mores peculiar to a given religion, such as the Judaeo-Christian commandments?

AB: I wouldn't want to exclude particular mores, but I am referring to a way of life which is more general and fundamental than specific actions. It seems that when a person is confronted by the complexity of his/her own existence and world, he/she needs somehow to organize an approach to them. Not to have such an organizational perspective leaves an individual open to chaos and disintegration from overexposure to sensations and experiences. An individual needs a worldview, a basic position regarding reality. The organization of experience which a worldview provides isn't merely a philosophical one. In many cases, human actions and reactions conceive an outlook on life before this is consciously verbalized. Worldview relates to the totality of a person and reflects his/her fundamental stance before life and experience. It is the lens through which experience is perceived.

RE: I would think that a person opting for religion would have a particular world view, one that is religious.

AB: Often this is true, and when it is, the religious worldview faces life with the expectation that there is meaning and purpose in human existence. This meaning and purpose is not circumscribed by man but transcends him . . . namely, "God." There are, of course, other views of the world which face life with the expectation that there is meaning. However, these hold that it is found totally in man and his world.

RE: How do you see this affecting living?

AB: As an organizing principle of life, a person's worldview shapes, and is shaped by, every action. So it is expected that a person's behaviors are consonant with his/her worldview. If a person has more or less consciously chosen a religious stance before life, normally, he/she will attempt to live by it. If a person has made this option within the framework of a particular religion's creed or cult, then, likewise, he/she will attempt to live according to these particulars. To do otherwise would be to verge on schizophrenia. It is on this basis that I see religious education as being, in part, a teaching for living. In other words, one major emphasis in religious education should be upon lifestyle behaviors.

RE: The choice of a worldview which is not religious also would suggest a need to live accordingly. In discussing lifestyle behaviors as a concern of religious education, wouldn't it be more on target to speak of teaching for *religious* living, teaching a *religious* lifestyle?

AB: I am presuming that the process of religious education concerns itself with those already acting within a religious worldview. I realize that, in some cases, this religious worldview is an implicit one. Within such a worldview all of living is religious. The fundamental stance toward life colors all subsequent behaviors and experiences. Life and the world within this perspective have religious connotations.

RE: One wonders if many learners within contemporary religious education operate from such a religious worldview.

AB: If not, then one of the purposes of religious education as teaching for living is to facilitate learners' formulation of such a worldview. In many cases this means helping them to discover what they implicitly hold.

RE: Teaching for living is a rather ambitious goal. Is this practical? Can *any* education achieve such a broad goal?

AB: I think that it is both practical and possible when one organizes what one means by lifestyle behaviors and then plans religious education accordingly.

RE: That sounds very similar to the goals of the moralist trend in religious education. This approach was, after all, concerned with the formation of piety and of religious behavior.

AB: In its *pure* form, the moralist view of religious education is concerned with the facilitation of piety, religious practice, and spiritual formation, but *only* with these. The goal of facilitating religious piety and practice and spiritual formation (for all its vagueness) is indeed congruent with a religious education which focuses upon teaching for living. Religious education, as an education in religion, is concerned with lifestyle behaviors.

RE: I find it difficult to see any clear difference in the moralist approach to lifestyle and your approach.

AB: Lifestyle is a total attribute of a person. It includes modes of thinking as well as modes of judging or of feeling. A lifestyle carries the configurations of one's understanding and knowledge just as living behaviors cannot help shaping both the extent and nature of understanding and knowledge. Lifestyle is a cumulative fusion of all those modes of acting and being which characterize one individual rather than another. Therefore, while we can distinguish teaching for lifestyle as *an* aspect of an education in religion, one cannot claim that this *is* religious education, nor that it is a discrete entity within it. Teaching for living and teaching for understanding and knowledge could be seen as dynamically intersecting so that organic unity results.

RE: Let's consider lifestyle behaviors for the present. You said, if I remember, that lifestyle is the "cumulative fusion of all those modes of acting and being which characterize the individual." That is at least as vague as "spiritual formation."

AB: Yes, I agree. However, what I propose is the formulation of some behavioral goals for religious education in lifestyle.

RE: What do you mean by behavioral goals?

AB: Let me answer that indirectly. Earlier in our conversation you noted that before undertaking any educational enterprise a teacher must know just what direction he/she hopes learning will take. In other words, there must be an overall objective for the whole enterprise and smaller goals for each stage of it. It is extremely difficult, and hardly efficient, to consider the manner in which one will reach an end before that end is clarified. Religious education, too, must have a clear objective and clear enroute goals. In the case where we have opted for an education *in* religion rather than for an education *about* religion, the objective of religious education is to facilitate religious living.

RE: Some task, considering that "religious living," like most general objectives, is open to all kinds of possible interpretations, some of which are conflicting.

AB: True. This demands that once the general objective has been formulated, the task of the religious educator is to describe more specifically what that objective will look like when it is achieved.

RE: Precisely! What does religious living, for example, look like in the lives of the learners concerned? What behaviors indicate religious living or what behaviors indicate otherwise?

AB: Or, from the educator's perspective, what exactly am I aiming to facilitate? How will I know if I have been successful? The answers to these questions will be learner behaviors which the teacher must then facilitate.

RE: Behavioral goals, then, don't necessarily describe course content.

AB: Right. They refer to the specific goals of a course in terms of the behaviors which the teacher will hope for from the learner. In relation to goals, behavior refers to specific actions by an individual, for example, spelling behaviors where a person proceeding through the necessary audio, oral, and/or writing activities, demonstrates that he can or cannot spell. Another example would be social behaviors, such as activities involved in meeting, greeting, communicating, and cooperating with others. As well as involving specific activities by the individual, behavior in this present sense also refers to any observable activity of the individual; jumping and singing are observable behaviors but we can also infer regarding a person's reading behaviors if, when confronting a text visually, he/she can, without prompting, enunciate it. A behavioral goal for a particular language class might be: when given a short written passage with related questions in French, the learner can demonstrate his/her ability to read and understand French by replying in English with appropriate answers.

RE: How does this apply to teaching for living? It seems that one difficulty in discussing lifestyle behaviors would be to discover behavioral goals for teaching which are "as large as life" and as sophisticated. It could be very easy to remain at a fairly crude level of behavioral goal-setting in this area.

AB: Benjamin Bloom, David Krathwohl and others have developed taxonomies giving cognitive and affective behaviors. Rodney Stark prepared a taxonomy of behaviors in the domain of religious experience and Charles Glock has added the five dimensions of ritualistic, ideological, intellectual, experiential, and consequential behaviors to that of religious experience. However, none of these incorporates behaviors which are specifically lifestyle oriented. Moreover by not being integrative these existing taxonomies emphasize a dichotomized human person.

RE: What, then, are the religious behaviors which religious education should facilitate?

AB: Simply stated, religious behaviors are behaviors which are consonant with a religious worldview. J. A. T. Robinson emphasized recently that there is not one set of behaviors in the human system which can be classified as pagan and another set which is strictly religious. It is our *patterning* of behaviors, our responses to different situations which testify to consistency or highlight its absence. For example, take laughing. To laugh in church during a service at the ongoing action could be quite areligious, even anti-religious. However, to laugh in church at a humorous point during the sermon, or to chuckle at the poorness of liturgical sense could stem directly from one's religious orientation.

RE: By "lifestyle" I understand those differences between us all in the day-to-day way in which we carry on living. For example, my lifestyle is different from my parents in that I like to entertain at home more, stay out later. I dress differently and have less money than they, and I tend to like variety in meals whereas their meals, by reason of health and habit, are generally plain and routine. Yet, my lifestyle is different again from that of those who socialize frequently, drink and smoke regularly, and live with great expense and mobility. These things would seem to be the usual understanding of "lifestyle."

AB: Does it really communicate much? Let's take two people who in this understanding seem to share a similar lifestyle: both are men, who eat simply, retire late at night and who are bearded and often bejeaned, even sharing the same brand name on their back pockets. What does that tell us about them? Such externals can convey messages about lifestyle which are as conflicting as "learners," "unreliable," "out to enjoy himself," "unorthodox," "one of the crowd," a friend or foe depending on one's attitude toward beards, jeans and late nighters. In fact, both gentlemen may be expressing similarily lifestyles which are dramatically different. To restrict lifestyle to differences in dress, timetable, habitat, etc., is to remain at a very superficial level.

RE: But don't individual expressions of taste such as dress, dwelling, occupation, and timetable belong to a person's lifestyle?

AB: Certainly, they are very much part of one's lifestyle. But the most dress tells us about a person is that he or she is wearing it. We can't even know whether it is worn from choice or from necessity. Externals are not a full indication of lifestyle and are open to much misinterpretation. The truer and, therefore, the more important elements are those which incline a person toward his choice of dress, dwelling, etc. The same decision could well be reached from very different starting points. It is these starting points which, being more accurate indications of lifestyle, deserve the attention of religious educators.

RE: Can you specify some of the indicators of lifestyle choices?

AB: Six elements present themselves as fundamental sources of a religious lifestyle: (1) holding a worldview which is religious; (2) formulating a personal story which is religious; (3) formulating values; (4) being moral; (5) relating with others; and (6) reacting to impersonal and interpersonal encounters. These behaviors don't occur along any continuum (chronological, qualitative, or quantitative), but, rather, the whole is more kaleidoscopic as all six interfuse with each other, affecting and being affected by each other. Yet, as processes, each does seem to have a separate identity. All aspects involve the total person, but where the thinking, feeling, and willing aspects of humanity end and begin in each of these areas is imprecise. Like lifestyle itself, these behaviors are essentially integrative. It is precisely for this reason that they can be useful to religious education.

RE: Earlier, when discussing worldview as a person's organizing principle, we mentioned that, possibly, many people do not possess a conscious worldview, religious or otherwise. This kind of unconsciousness leaves room for inconsistencies and contradictions in our various behaviors, a kind of "say one thing and do another" lifestyle.

AB: While this is true, the demands of life often force us to reexamine our worldview from time to time. It is in those instances of unconsciousness and reexamination that religious education would seem to have a role: to facilitate the formulation and discovery of a religious worldview. In this the probability that the learners may opt for a worldview different from the religious educator's must always be recognized.

RE: As a behavioral goal, to use your terms, this correlates the completed amount of religious education with a more conscious religious worldview. In other words, upon completion of x amount of religious education, learners will have a stronger and more explicit faith commitment. How will the religious educator know this has occurred?

AB: While a person's religious worldview or faith can't be directly measured or assessed, it can be inferred from behavioral expressions of a particular stance. Offering opportunities for learners to try formulating for themselves their own position concerning faith is both process-content and product-content. The attempt to make such formulations is a highly personal event and extreme care should be taken that the privacy and freedom of the learner are safeguarded. Formal opportunities for expression of this private and personal formulation should be rare. The religious educator's task is to facilitate this formulation chiefly by offering informed and comprehensive outlooks on life, on religion, and the options offered by other worldviews. Teaching for a religious worldview varies greatly with the maturity of the learners involved. At a *conscious* level such formulation seems to be more the task of adulthood, not childhood.

RE: What about the second lifestyle behavior which you mentioned: formulating a personal story?

AB: What the worldview is to the person for the whole of existence the personal story is for one's specific existence. How does one see him/herself and his/her experiences so far? Is there a thread running through one's years? The personal story is the individual's personal pulling together of life's events and situations in order to make of them a meaningful whole.

The formulation of the personal story is the story of the self as it emerges continually in a person's history. For the person who has chosen a religious worldview, the personal story is a religious one. If we are areligious in our bearing toward human history and existence, it would be reasonable to expect a similar agnosticism toward our own particular history and existence. On the other hand, the personal story of faith can influence the subsequent development of that story. The person who sees his/her life as one touched by the graciousness of a loving God will be more positive toward himself in the future than one who sees life as meaningless or as totally dependent on oneself.

RE: It would seem that facilitating a person's ongoing formulation of his/her lifestyle could include studies of other persons and other groups, of scripture and of church history. It certainly could provide the learner with an informed perspective with which to confront his contemporary position and the position of the religious group to which he may belong. Since liturgy and prayer express this relationship to the group and a person's life story, religious education would include learning to improve such expressions.

AB: Yes, and it would also seem helpful to this aspect of lifestyle to focus more directly upon the self, through study of the psyche and of human relations.

The third selected aspect of lifestyle behaviors was formulating values. As Sidney Simon has clearly explained, values have certain definite characteristics. They are freely chosen, with the emphasis on both "free" and "chosen." Because of the consciousness required for such a definite choice, values are principles, people, or things toward which we have indicated not only agreement and preference but sufficient attraction to choose them over other things and to demonstrate these choices in our behavior. They are also very personal and demand a high degree of personal involvement in their selecting.

RE: As with worldview, I am sure, many of us have "values" which are with us from habit more than from conscious choice. Many of us have half-thought out, half-chosen values, sometimes in collision with each other because they have not been brought into consciousness. Probably we are capable only of holding very few values at any given time.

AB: Because of the conscious choice involved in them, values are relatively stable. They are not totally unchanging, or unchangeable but are products of our situations, our times and our reactions within these. This is another aspect of the personal quality of values. I cannot choose values for another, no matter how much I care for either the other or the particular values. Nevertheless, we often value things because significant people in our lives value them. Value education attempts to provide opportunities for practice in making and living conscious value choices. It also focuses upon educating the learner of any age in the *value-making process*. Rather than take several highly desirable elements and attempt to impress learners that these are highly desirable, value education tries to educate persons to make their own value choices.

RE: A parallel seems to exist in that Confucian saying: "Give a man a fish and you feed him for a day; teach him how to fish and you feed him for life."

AB: Yes, paraphrasing we could say: "Give a person your values and he can act during childhood; teach a person to choose his own values and he can continue choosing throughout his life."

RE: So many of our decisions in life seem to be options by default; we end up in one position because we didn't opt for another. Yet, value-making and value-living seem integral to any lifestyle particularly to a religious one. This brings us to the fourth lifestyle behavior: being moral. Do you see this as different from having values?

AB: Being moral could well be classified as the living out

of our values. Our relationships and our reactions seem also to be the embodiments of our values. This underscores the need for consistency between them. Like values, morality has much to do with personal choices and their outcomes. At the simplest level, morality may be described as our selection of behaviors. Obviously, some behaviors are more significant than others in this process. The child who pulls the cat's tail may be described in terms having immoral, if not amoral, overtones, as naughty. Such behavior hardly matches in moral significance that, for example, of foolish and irresponsible driving.

Kohlberg, for example, has explicated six different levels of morality which he describes as consecutive and progressive stages. He argues that the ability to make moral decisions is developmental. Consequently, moral behavior is determined by the cognitive understanding of the principle of justice which the particular individual possesses.

RE: Well, it seems to me that the goal of a religious education certainly would be to foster the development of moral thinking and behaviors. So, models of morality which are close to the learner, but on the next higher level, should be put before learners to challenge their own response. It also seems that, like value education, moral education would strive to help the learner choose his own behaviors, that is, to practice morality rather than to learn about it. Moreover, any serious education in morality would study the social and personal consequences of certain actions so that decisions could be informed choices.

AB: I believe this kind of moral education would be more effective and simpler to achieve if accompanied by a focus on education in the other behaviors that are also part of lifestyle: worldview, personal story, and values. The final two sets of behaviors which it seems to me create an overall lifestyle are relationships and reactions. It seems almost axiomatic to observe that relationships are a very important part of an individual's lifestyle. This area includes those with whom one forms relationships, the nature of those relationships, the number of any given kind of relationships, and their maintenance or termination. There is an obvious enough interfusion between values, morality, and relationships. The manner and motive for beginning, maintaining, or severing relationships involve attitudes toward others, their rights, needs, and obligations. The care with which a relationship is pursued will vary greatly depending on its place in one's worldview and values, and the experience within one's personal history of love and concern for another. Furthermore, one's personal orientation as well as one's worldview influence what is looked for in a relationship.

Reactions seem to belong to both the intellectual and to the affective sphere. There can be heavily-charged reactions which are aroused by intellectual points of differences or similarities as well as those aroused on an emotional level. Reactions can also take their shape from previous experiences. Something happens, we react one way or another. How we react cannot but be influenced by our values, our moral code, our relationships, our consciousness, and our perspective on life. Probably even more important, with time our reactions form patterns, even habits. Are these patterns consistent with our worldview? Our story? Our values? Do they harm or help our relationships?

Religious education in lifestyle needs to help learners raise these questions for themselves, attempt to answer them and work toward an integral and religious lifestyle. This is not an education for children alone, nor even primarily for children.

RE: We have said already that religion expresses itself in behaviors and in lifestyle. The elements which energize a particular lifestyle you understand to be worldview, personal story, values, morality, relationships, and reactions. Consequently, to facilitate these is a fitting goal for religious education as teaching for living. But, do you mean that there are *no* specific values, worldview, relationships, and so on, which you see as having to be communicated through religious education?

AB: That depends on what you mean by "having to be communicated." It is not a matter of a teacher handing over a set of facts or beliefs which the learner assimilates and turns back as *the* religious worldview, personal story, morality, etc. In the first place, each of these elements which I have isolated as aspects of a person's lifestyle is something which cannot be transmitted. Rather, each of them is the result of the individual's working his/her own personal experiences into a personal lifestyle.

The facts, beliefs of others, opinions, history, reasons in favor or against a particular value, for example, may be presented to a person. It can even be imposed by some use of moral pressure, but unless the individual chooses such a value for him/herself, then, it is of no real value to him/her.

RE: So you don't advocate a teaching of a specific lifestyle. What do you advocate as appropriate to religious education?

AB: I strongly advocate education in choosing or building a lifestyle by forming values, worldview, morality, relationships, history, and reactions. These elements are an important aspect of an individual's lifestyle but only if the individual can choose them for him/herself. The alternative is not the choice of, for example, "bad" values, but the *failure to choose* values or lifestyle at all . . . a kind of deadness.

RE: Does that mean that a learner might well choose undesirable living patterns? Irreligious values, say?

AB: I suppose that that is always the risk. Religious education which emphasizes teaching for living should assist persons to clarify their worldview and integrate and formulate their own personal history. This personal story and worldview are expressions of an individual's faith. Like values, only the individual can express this for himself.

RE: What about morality? Is there no morality which is religious or decidedly irreligious?

AB: Very definitely there is morality which is consistent with a religious worldview. The Christian religion, for example, takes its stance toward life based upon the belief that human existence finds its fullness in Jesus Christ who revealed to men a God of love and who said: "By this shall all men know that you are my disciples that you have love one for the other." For the Christian, there is a very definite morality of love. However, one cannot force these things on anyone. To respect both the person and the morality, even the Christian ethic must be freely chosen. Even the form and expression of love is impossible to define. It is the individual's response in love which will determine what form the action/word/silence takes. To prescribe a certain behavior as loving is both unnecessary and dangerous. The result can be a kind of legalism toward fulfilling the prescribed act with an ever-retreating personal involvement in it. Another shortcoming of such prescription is to limit the creativity and responsiveness of people who can easily come to trust the law more than their own hearts. It is likewise for relationships and reactions: each of which is intensely personal, even while being very social. One cannot relate nor react for someone else, or even as someone else would. Education can help people in working these things out by helping them to learn their own responses.

RE: This is all great, but how do you see it being effected in practice?

AB: First of all, I do not understand teaching as a process of transmitting truths from one person to another, nor learning as the absorption of something from someone else. Learning is coming to know how to find things out, where to find them out, how to reason, choose, and act. Learning is a very broad term, including all the changes in all kinds of behavior in an individual. There needs to be a readiness on the part of the learner. But there also needs to be involvement as people learn best by doing. We must remember that the learner of whatever age is always *IN PROCESS*. We can always assume that the religious education in which we are engaging is not the only religious education in this person's life.

Before planning any venture in religious education as teaching for living, the teacher must investigate four key areas of concern: the learner, the subject matter, the environment in which learning should optimally occur, and one's own behaviors in teaching. Whether planning for a whole program or for a single session, the teacher would do well to answer the following questions. First, in regard to the learner: where is the learner *now* with respect to religious lifestyle? Where does he/she need to go next? What learning is he/she capable of or ready for now? What behaviors can be reasonably expected at the conclusion of this program or session?

Secondly, as regards the subject matter: What is it to be? What is most suitable or necessary or urgent for the learner at this stage? How can I best teach this material? How much? How quickly? What sequence? What medium?

Thirdly, as regards the teaching environment: what physical, social, emotional, and intellectual environment will best enable learners to assimilate and integrate this material? What environmental effects could be harmful? How much is realistically possible?

Finally, as regards the teacher's own behaviors: How can I best facilitate learning in this situation? Can I do it alone? If not, with whom? What is needed in preparation for teaching? How will my behavior assist the learners?

Briefly stated, teaching for living demands an educational approach to religious education which is personal, integrative, informative and yet, experiential rather than transmissive. It requires an atmosphere which is warm, open, and respectful of both teachers and product-content.

RE: Is such a religious education possible?

AB: Not only possible but probable when religious educators are aware of and prepared for conducting such programs. Hopefully, the next chapters of this book will increase this awareness and encourage preparation and continual updating along these lines.

II

Teaching for Learning

There is probably nothing as anxiety-provoking as the thought of change. And yet, in important areas of concern, change occurs so gradually that, oftentimes, it is accomplished and new directions have been taken, before we are aware of the process. Reflection upon the past fifty-year history of the church and the nation will verify this statement.

Change, or the ability to change, is a vital sign for any group which itself is the agent for change, that is, when it is actively involved in establishing its goals and determining the directions in which it wills to move. On the other hand, change, or the ability to change, does not augur for success if the group is merely the passive recipient of decisions imposed upon it by forces outside itself. Again, reflection will attest that many of the major crises in recent history have been rooted in this dynamic. If this is true of the past, it is even more so today as our society, our cultural mores, and our economic structures continue to shape our environment and create a climate in which the achievement of Christian living becomes more difficult.

The recognition of the realities of this situation is a challenge to religious educators who strive to teach the gospel message as the mainstay of the Christian way of life. The challenge is greater today than it has ever been before because Christian moral values—gospel values—openly conflict with social behaviors which have been endorsed by the highest court in the country. Suddenly, even though the winds of change had been prevalent for a decade, the Christian finds himself *free* to opt for that which is legally correct but morally unacceptable. This dilemma is augmented by the fact that renewal in the church and the mobility of our society have eliminated many of the supports which fortified the Christian of yesteryear. No longer do Christians usually live in the shadow of their church; no longer is the pastor regarded as the arbitor of religious, social and/or moral conflicts; and thinking no longer reflects a siege mentality.

This situation is alarming in a sense and, if viewed merely as a problem, could dissipate much of our psychic strength. On the other hand, it can serve as a stimulus, challenging us to use all of our creative energies to formulate and implement a response which will have positive impact upon the Christian community. In doing so, the religious educator is a change agent, assisting others in their efforts toward personal freedom, namely, free to live the gospel message and to form their own moral value system rather than be shaped by the oppressive values of a materialistic society.

But, let us look at where we are that we might use the best of what we have in designing a process for the future.

One might be tempted to describe the situation in religious education today as organized confusion. Organized because in several parishes throughout the country serious attempts are being made to design curricula to meet the religious educational needs of the people of God. Confusion because at this point in time there seems to be no emerging pattern to provide direction for the future. Texts, which incorporated the principles of Vatican II,

together with insights from latest theological, psychological, and sociological thinking are assailed at almost every
turn. The criticisms being bandied about reverberate
throughout the Christian community. How often have we
heard these and other similar remarks: "Children do not
know their religion"; "It is impossible to convey religious/
spiritual values to a people engrossed in a materialistic
society"; "New texts are inadequate because they necessitate
a sharing of one's own personal spiritual values and most
religion teachers are just too uncomfortable doing that";
and perhaps, most frequently, "Let's get back to the basics."

A religious educator might well become dispirited in view
of these criticisms unless he/she sensitizes him/herself to the
fact that they are often made by those who are looking over
their shoulder to the unquestioned and unquestionable
programs in the pre-Vatican II era; by those who dissipate
so much energy honing in on the "good old days" that they
are blinded to the significant signs of the times today. More
than ever before, religious educators are being challenged
to break through the apathy of the silent majority and to
actively demonstrate, perhaps like the prophets of the Old
Testament, that effective religious instruction does not
occur in the vacuum of a once-a-week program, but rather
at all levels of the lived Christian experience.

This challenge is, moreover, rooted in the gospel design
for teaching religion. This design is evidenced in the Christian philosophy of life as it was lived and expressed in the
early Christian communities. These communities, formed
and supported by the earliest followers of Christ, most
certainly were permeated with religious experiences intended to impart the Christian message. It is unimaginable
that the leaders of these communities had in mind anything
but the total commitment of the community to the princi-

ples of the gospel. So, too, today's religious educators must consciously shape a climate for the effective teaching of the gospel. They must also demonstrate concern that teaching occur, not only in the context of the acquisition of religious knowledge, but also that knowledge be so assimilated by individuals and by the Christian community that they too may give witness to a Christian commitment in their daily lives.

Basically, most religious educators agree with the premise that they are called upon to teach the gospel message. Despite this consensus, however, the situation indicates that, in recent years, they have, in fact, been preoccupied with changing theological themes, and been caught up, as it were, with educational gimmicks, i.e., games, A-V materials, role playing, and the like—these materials, at times, becoming the program itself. In other words, process becomes the program (product).

While it is readily admitted that there is a place for the good process in religious instruction, particularly since it is so much a part of the secular education scene, caution must be exercised that it is not employed in a hit or miss schedule and without a theoretical base. For example, the use of a filmstrip serves no practical purpose unless it reinforces the concepts expressed in the performance objectives. On the other hand, the use of a purely pedantic, theoretical approach, lacking in practical dimensions, is lost on students nurtured in a multisensual academic milieu. It is necessary to avoid both extremes. It would seem that an integration of theory and practice is essential in any program of positive action designed not only to impart religious knowledge but to stimulate the assimilation of knowledge into a Christian philosophy of life.

It is against the backdrop of the foregoing that the following questions are explored: What are the gospel dimensions of teaching? How can teachers teach for learning and for living? How can teachers teach for learning today for living in the church of tomorrow? We will address these questions by presenting a teaching model, henceforward to be referred to as the Cove model, which incorporates four fundamental aspects of the teaching-learning situation. As stated previously, the religious educator must shape the climate for effective teaching-learning and in the doing must incorporate the four C's of a meaningful program. The four C's include: C_1 (commitment), C_2 (consistency), C_3 (cooperation), C_4 (communication). We will further propose that all these elements have a theoretical and practical dimension within the framework of the teaching model which is designed to remove the "fuzzies" from the teaching of religion. Indeed, a brief overview of the New Testament will reveal that these elements—commitment, consistency, cooperation, and communication—were evident in the teaching mission of Christ.

The gospel accounts of the teaching Jesus describe a man committed to the proclamation of a specific message: evil overcome. Matthew writes: "He taught in their synagogues, proclaimed the good news of the Kingdom, and cured the people of every disease and illness" (4:23). He spoke with the authority of the Son of God but chose, nonetheless, to demonstrate his commitment by his way of life. It is, therefore, not surprising, as McKenzie notes, that the title "teacher" was most often conferred upon Jesus.[1]

Although scriptural scholars disagree as to the exact meaning of each of the parables, it seems obvious that the intention of Jesus was to use an approach that would help the people understand the substance of his message. "By means of many such parables, he taught them the message in a way they could understand" (Mk 4:33).

Christ used the parables as a means to an end. They were used to inform as well as to stimulate his audience to inquire about their meaning that he might through dialogue explicate the meaning of the law. Jesus communicated, however, more than a content message. It was a challenge to a people devoted to what was to them a meticulous observance of the Mosaic Law; to focus on the spirit rather than the letter of the law; to incorporate his message into their daily lives; to seek a deeper purpose in life. While it is true that the Hebrew faith, like the Christian faith, has its ultimate end in union with the Father, Christ's appeal was for a turning from service through fear of the Father toward service through love of the Father. Before Christ could show them the way to the Father, they must respond effectively to his message and this response was predicated upon intimate trust (or cooperation). In a conscious effort to reveal the Father, Jesus taught by virtue of his authority, and he asked for a response, a commitment, to the New Law of love.

Christ's impact upon the people of his time was revolutionary insofar as he introduced the (New) Law. However, his constant referral to the Old Law, his insistence upon its observance was reassuring to devout Jews. Over and over again he pointed out the consistency of his message with the Mosaic Law. Any apparent inconsistency was with the burdensome interpretations that had been imposed by their spiritual leadership. For those who were committed to the will of the Father, Christ's message posed no problem in contradiction.

The timeless message of Jesus continues to relate to those who wish to hear and to accept the challenge. However, just as Jesus spoke to the people of his day within the context of their ability to understand, and in settings appropriate to their culture, it has been essential to adapt the message to the cultural differences among people from the Pauline era to the present. Indeed, failure in sensitivity to cultural differences could spell the difference between "listening to" and "hearing" the word. Sensitivity is the key to establishing the climate.

This need to be aware of the culture, albeit a local culture, is reflected in much that has been written to stimulate a renewed interest in teaching the gospel message. The document on *The Church Today* from the Second Vatican Council reflects the cultural dimension of the gospel. It states, "Let them blend modern science and its theories and the understanding of the most recent discoveries with Christian morality and doctrine. Thus their religious practice and morality can keep pace with their scientific knowledge and with an ever-advancing technology. Thus, too, they will be able to test and interpret all things in a truly Christian spirit."[2]

Perhaps on a more concrete level, the General Catechetical Directory reinforces the same theme. "The summit and center of catechetical formation lies in an aptitude and ability to communicate the gospel message. This formation requires, therefore, an accurate formation in theological doctrine, in anthropology, and in methodology, geared to the level of knowledge that is to be attained."[3] And again, the American bishops' pastoral *To Teach As Jesus Did* which set the tone as it were for Catholic education in our day, calls upon religious educators to be aware of and concerned about those scientific and social factors which influence the people of God in the modern world.

Convention speakers and keynoters at workshops designed to generate enthusiasm for teaching the gospel message even on the local parish level are fond of quoting the Vatican documents, the pastoral and other sources. While these documents do provide an important thrust for religious education, they, like the impressive speakers who sincerely promulgate them, all too often leave the religious educator in the same old quandary: How does one apply the message from convention hall to the parish center? It is all too apparent that something is lost in the translation to the reality of the parish scene.

The goal of religious education is to prepare individuals for Christian living. Again looking to the gospels, it is evident that Jesus taught a way of life expressed in charity, peace, justice, and reconciliation. He, in a sense, threw down the gauntlet challenging the people of his day to a renewed way of life. The message of the gospel hurls out that same challenge today, that is, to adopt a lifestyle that is truly Christian in all its dimensions. To communicate the gospel design effectively, it must be taught not simply as a content to be understood but as a life to be lived. Thus, the teacher of religion must be conscious of two important contents, namely, product-content and process-content.

James Michael Lee notes that in teaching religion there are eight major substantive contents;[4] however, for our purposes we will discuss two of these contents, product-content and process-content. Let us explore these concepts. The teacher plans the content for a given session, for example the parable of the Good Samaritan, compares the qualities of care and concern evident in it to the care and concern Christ demonstrated in his life, and makes a practical application to the day to day Christian life experience. This is the content the teacher intends that the learner will learn and assimilate into his/her Christian value system. In other words, this content will produce change and, hence, is called the product-content. However, every teacher will agree that this product-content must be taught in an atmosphere which reflects care and concern for everyone who is part of the teaching-learning situation. That atmosphere does not just happen. It often calls for a great deal more expertise and effort on the part of the teacher than does the planning of the product-content because unlike the product-content which can be predetermined, there is no way that the teacher can anticipate the many different factors which might affect teaching-learning outcomes. Thus, the teacher must be sensitive to these factors and be flexible enough to control the situations. It is through this flexibility in controlling the atmosphere that the teacher creates the climate. Shaping the climate is a continuing, interactive dynamic. It is an ongoing process throughout the teaching-learning experience. Hence, it is the process-content.

Both these contents, product-content and process-content, are equally important and both must be thoroughly integrated if one hopes to teach religion effectively. Nevertheless, the teacher must be very conscious of the distinction between the two. If the teacher is teaching only product-content, then the teaching of lifestyle behaviors would not be rooted in a creed. The substance of the creed is the product-content. The faith experience and the sharing of the religious expression of faith is the process-content. Lest there be any confusion, process-content does not refer to the use of A-V and other materials, however useful they might be in a specific experience, but refers specifically to shaping the climate for a faith response in order that the product-content might find meaningful expression in a life to be lived.

In order to effectively employ both product-content and

process-content there is a need to appreciate and understand the role of theory and practice as it relates to religious
education. Through an understanding of theory and its
relationship to practice, a religious educator can better
facilitate the skills for the teaching-learning act which em-
braces both product-content and process-content. It is then,
through the fruitful integration of product-content and
process-content, that the conditions are present for Christian lifestyle objectives to be obtained.

There is a need for both theory and practice in all teaching, and this is also true for the teaching of religion. However, the integration of theory and practice is difficult, if not
impossible, unless the religious educator is operating out of
a teaching theory that includes both. Toffler seemed to be
referring to this need to be grounded in a theory of teaching which includes theory and practice when he wrote,
"Learning under conditions of high novelty requires us to
move back and forth between theory and practice, between
classroom and community, faster and more frequently than
ever before."[5] It is in the "back and forthness" that theory
lends predictability to the teaching process and practice
helps to concretize theory.

Although this is true that there is a need for both theory
and practice, yet often it seems that the one problem with
theories is that they are too theoretical. Nevertheless,
theories are essential in order to build good models for
teaching. Smith provides some basic criteria for a teaching
theory:

  a) a statement of variables comprising teacher be-
     havior
  b) a formulation of possible relations among the var-
     iables
  c) hypothesis about the relations between the variables

comprising teaching behavior and variables descriptive of the psychological and social conditions within which teaching behavior occurs.[6]

A good teaching theory can be helpful in providing models which in turn help to clarify the theory. The model in turn brings clarity and vision to the teaching experience. To explicate, let us look at the Popham and Baker model.

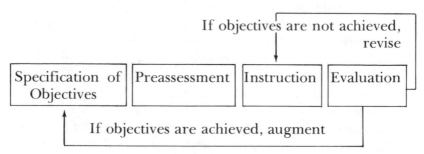

If objectives are not achieved, revise

| Specification of Objectives | Preassessment | Instruction | Evaluation |

If objectives are achieved, augment

The four components of this model can be explained in the following fashion:

1) the objectives are specified in terms of learner behavior;
2) the learner is preassessed in regards to the specific objective;
3) the instructional activities are designed to bring about the intended objective; and
4) the learner's attainment of the objectives is evaluated.

After these steps are completed, the teacher then either returns to Step 1, or, if the objectives were not attained, the teacher returns to Step 3 to revise the instruction.[7] The main focus of this particular model is directed to the learner rather than centered upon the teacher. On the other hand, it also does not include a process for shaping the environment, which is important for the effective teaching of religion.

The model offered by James Michael Lee, though more complex in structural design, places a great deal of emphasis upon the importance of the environment, the teacher, subject matter, as well as the learner, all of which elements are intimately interrelated in the teaching-learning act. The Lee model is shown as it appears in *The Flow of Religious Instruction.*[8]

The key for this model is as follows: (T) teacher; (L) learner; (E) environment; and (SM) subject matter. The shaded E comprises the environment which covers the entire learning situation. In this model the learner (L) assumes a pivotal position around which the teaching and learning activity are designed in order to achieve the stated goal. For further purposes of clarity, the teacher (T) is placed outside the model which attests to the fact that the teacher is "the constant structurer of the learning situation."[9] The teacher then specifies the goals to be attained and, within the learning situation, makes the necessary adjustments to achieve

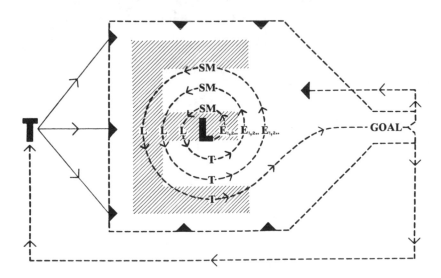

the goal. The E represented by E_1, E_2, . . . designates special aspects of the environment, namely, field trips, media, and the physical setting. As in the Popham and Baker model, if the goal is not attained, then the teacher reconstructs the teaching-learning activity and conversely if the goal is ascertained, other goals are considered in a specific process involving the learner.

Both the Popham-Baker and the Lee models are applicable to the teaching of religion. However, because, as stated previously, we are convinced that teaching religion is a unique experience based on the components of commitment, consistency, cooperation, and communication, it is within this framework that we propose a model which places emphasis upon their inclusion in the teaching-learning experience.

The framework for this model is the shaded C; only within the C do the other components have meaning; for purposes of brevity it shall be referred to as the Cove model. By way of explanation, C refers to the climate which is necessarily generated in every teaching-learning experi-

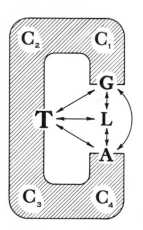

ence. The climate is contingent upon the four C's (commitment, consistency, cooperation, and communication) hence their placement within the shaded C. T represents the teacher who controls the climate but is at the same time a very important part of it. G refers to the goal which the teacher determines through interaction with the learner L, the focal point of the model. A symbolizes the activity of the teaching-learning experience and is designed not only to meet the needs of the learner (L) but also leads to the realization of the goal (G). The curved lines T-G and T-A are indicative of the fact that the goal and the activity must be flexible if there is to be any surety that learning is to occur. In reality, no teaching takes place unless learning also takes place. For this reason all vectors point in both directions, indicating the interaction necessary in every facet of the model. The teacher structures the goal to meet the needs of the learner, and with both in mind directs the activity of the teaching-learning experience to provide a climate in which religious education can be realized.

The crux of the Cove model is the climate. The teacher shapes the climate for effective teaching-learning with the learner (L) the pivotal or central focus of the process. While this is the basic premise of the model, it is not meant to imply that the learner does not do much to shape the climate, a fact to which anyone with even minimal experience in teaching will attest. What is implied is that, in shaping the climate, the teacher must be sensitive to the particular needs of the learner. The teacher by virtue of his/her role assumes responsibility for others in the learning situation. However, neither teacher nor learner funcions in a vacuum. The teacher, in structuring the climate, must consciously strive to involve the learner in such a way as to guarantee that maximum learning will occur with minimum anxiety.

As each teacher and learner enters the learning situation, they bring with them a personal history which includes not only the relevant past but also the dynamic present. Each also brings specific expectations for the immediate experience and, usually, residual hope for the future. Aware of this, the teacher must be prepared to adapt a well-thought-out and thoroughly prepared agenda to a climate which may be very different from that which was anticipated. Unless the teacher has this flexibility, this talent for coping with and restructuring the climate on the spot, then all the well-prepared lessons in the world will not result in teaching-learning situations.

Shaping the climate cannot be achieved without following some basic guidelines which we here suggest. First, the teacher must make a conscious effort not to impose his/her personal history, attendant with all its attitudes and values, upon the learner when structuring the climate. Secondly, the teacher must be aware of, or sensitive to, the fact that each learner has his/her own personal history which may be uniquely different, not only from the teacher's, but also from every other learner in a given situation. Thirdly, the teacher must be ever on the alert for the cues that the learner gives off during the teaching-learning act as to the effect of the general climate upon him/her as person. This is not a list in descending order of importance. A failure on the part of the teacher to note the cues could mean failure to shape the climate and to achieve the goal. As a matter of fact, when this happens, the goal has replaced the learner as the focal point of the teaching-learning dynamic.

Let us concretize the guidelines with a practical example. The teacher may have spent several hours preparing a lesson to teach the concept of God, our loving Father. In preparing the lesson, he/she may have recalled many personal experiences in his/her background with his/her own father which reinforced the idea that one aspect of fatherhood is the benevolent care of children. Such reminiscence may even result in a rather happy and serene attitude about fatherhood in general and God in particular. In this aura, the teacher enters the teaching-learning situation in which some, perhaps many, learners have not had this personal good-father relationship. In any event, the learners enter the situation "cold." If the teacher is unaware of this as he/she sets out to establish the tone, shape the climate, he/she may begin to generate undertones of resentment among learners who, first of all, cannot identify with benevolent fatherhood and, secondly, begin to be uncomfortable because they cannot do so. The cues which indicate that this is happening may range from a restlessness to "stalking out" behavior depending upon the age of the learner. In either event, learning does not occur. A sensitive teacher will pick up the undertones and will immediately begin to structure a climate in which the learner is more receptive to the concept of the fatherhood of God. The only other alternative is to redefine the goal. While this may be highly desirable in some instances, if it occurs too often, one sacrifices program for happenstance.

It is precisely in the structuring of the climate that the four C's proposed in the model are essential. The four C's, as mentioned previously, are commitment, consistency, cooperation, and communication. These four elements help to fashion the climate (C) which is necessary for the effective and meaningful teaching of religion.

Commitment on the part of the teacher is basic. Unless the teacher demonstrates an awareness of the gospel message and incorporates a gospel dimension in shaping the climate, he/she is a contradiction to the principles and concepts he/she is attempting to communicate, and Christian living outcomes may not be realized. This paradox has all too often provided a stumbling block in the teaching-learning situation especially as it applies to the basic gospel message from which the learner draws the criteria against which he/she will make a personal commitment to a Christian way of life. For religious educators, commitment calls for a high correspondence between the individual's goals and the gospel goals. This accord will prove a stabilizing force in living the Christian message not only in our day but also in the future. In short, if the teacher is truly committed, then his/her commitment is an integral part of the climate.

The second C of the climate is consistency. Used in the context of the model, consistency includes accountability. The teacher is accountable not only to him/herself but also to the learner. In general, teachers are accountable to themselves in that they must frequently evaluate where they are in light of what they are doing, and accountable to the learners in that they must continually shape the climate for the most effective teaching-learning situation. If there is harmony between who the teacher is and what he/she is doing, then this is projected into the teaching-learning climate and frees the teacher, as it were, to concentrate on the learner, the goal, the activity and to make whatever adjustments are necessary to affect Christian learning outcomes. The teacher's freedom to do this lends consistency to the process, and the learner is then free to become truly involved in establishing the goals, selecting the activity, and structuring the climate.

The third C is cooperation which reminds the teacher that the teaching-learning situation is only one part, sometimes a very small part, of the learner's day. If the dichotomy between the teaching-learning situation and the "real life" situation is too great, then the carry-over is apt to be minimal. In every teaching-learning situation there is an inherent need to cooperate with parents, other teachers, administrators and concerned adults. Religious educators cannot function effectively without the cooperation of others. Therefore, to structure a climate that relates to the reality of the parish scene, the teacher can probably best demonstrate leadership by seeking the cooperation of all involved in the educational process. The need for cooperation between the teacher and the learner is obvious, and it would appear to be unnecessary to belabor the point. Moreover, if there is good communication, then teacher-learner cooperation exists as a natural consequence.

Communication has been relegated to the fourth C, not because it is any way less important, but because it is easier to talk about communication than it is to communicate. For this reason, we chose to discuss this fourth 'C' in greater detail. We have been stressing the importance of structuring the climate of the teaching-learning situation in order that the teacher may more effectively communicate the gospel message. It is then the responsibility of the teacher to develop skills in listening, questioning and responding that will encourage the learner to ask questions, to interact with others, to express his ideas and ideals, and to come to an awareness that one need not have all the answers to live comfortably in a climate structured for Christian living outcomes. A teacher exercising these skills can effectively facilitate teaching-learning activities and, in the doing, structure a climate for communicating Christian values and behaviors. More specific comment will be made regarding these when addressing the need to create a climate.

In almost every field of endeavor, education, industry, the professions, there has been a concentration on group dynamics, sensitivity sessions and the like. While there is no intention to undermine the importance and usefulness of these programs, one is sometimes tempted to ask how people who spend so much time learning how to communicate find time to communicate. Much attention has been given to the importance of both verbal (oral and/or written) and nonverbal (body language) communication. Skill in nonverbal communication is important. The teacher should be aware not only of the signals given out to convey his/her affective state, but should also be alert to pick up the clues from the learner. Sometimes, the ability to recognize the signal and to communicate understanding and acceptance of the learner's affective state is the most meaningful experience in the teaching-learning situation. However, it would seem somewhat beyond the scope and intention of this book to elaborate on the subject in greater detail.

Verbal communication can often be a much more difficult medium of expression. One major erroneous assumption is that we really say what we mean when talking with another. A second is that the person really hears what we are saying. While this confusion in social situations may or may not have negative consequences, it would appear to be a luxury we cannot afford in the teaching-learning situation. It should be even less tolerated since it can be avoided as the following discussion will demonstrate.

The affective aspect of the teaching-learning situation has for years been the focus of much of the literature relating to education. *Death At An Early Age,* while probably not the first attack on the strictly cognitive approach to learning was certainly the most dramatic. John Holt's *Why Children Fail,* and the numerous works on humanistic education, have pointed out the devastating effect on learners in any teaching-learning situation when the transmission of facts is the pivotal concern. The affective domain applied to the teaching-learning situation refers equally to the teacher as well as to the learner. Because so much is available on the subject as it relates to the learner, we would like to emphasize that the affect, i.e., feelings, emotions, and desires of the teacher are of equal importance. A failure to realize this, a failure on the part of the teacher to spend some time in determining his/her affective state, could prove to be the most negative factor in the teaching-learning experience. This applies not only to the general situation but to the specific as well. Before assuming the role of a teacher in religious education the individual must examine whether or not one's personal value system is in conflict with the learner. For example, there are many well-intentioned and dedicated people who could not and should not attempt to function in the socio-economic milieu of minority groups. The ability to relate to one's affective state is in Morton Kelsey's view characteristic of a mature person. He states, "The mature person knows his own hostility; he may not always succeed, but he at least tries to use it as a creative person."[10] If the person is functioning in a climate that does not generate value conflict, he/she must also be attuned to the affective aspect of a specific session. A few moments spent in determining his/her emotional state before a given session should enable the teacher to be more empathic toward the learners. Thomas B. Gregory points out that a teacher deals with affect in two general ways: (1) he/she maintains an ongoing attitude of support, positive regard, and personal concern for the students; (2) the teacher is not reluctant to discuss the students' affective concerns whenever they assume dominance of their thought and behavioral processes; in such cases the teacher allows affect to become the subject matter (content) of the lesson.[11] The

Cove model proposed in this chapter is rooted in this concept. It is the identification of the learner's needs, whether cognitive or affective, and the structuring of the climate in which learning will occur that set the stage for effective teaching and learning.

There are obstacles to the empathic relationship described on the part of both teacher and learner. One of the most obvious is the mental set of the teacher and learner. If the teacher has predetermined expectations as to the learner's behavior and/or abilities; if the teacher brings to the situation the residual effect of preceding experiences; if the teacher is present at, rather than present to the situation; if the teacher is incapable of experiencing unconditional positive personal regard for each learner as a unique individual, then an empathic relationship is impossible. This is true in the converse situation, namely, learner to teacher. Assuming that the teacher can add this dimension to the teaching-learning situation, there are nevertheless certain skills which facilitate the teaching-learning process. It is not our intention to add to the plethora of material available on the subject of communication skills. However, it is worthwhile to attend to three skills which are essential to an empathic relationship, namely, questioning, listening, and responding.

What are the best questions to ask and how should we ask them? It has been said that the best questions start with these words: who, what, when, where, why, and how. Questions beginning with these words give the learners an opportunity to express their thinking beyond the unproductive "yes" and "no" responses. In this manner the teacher can avoid questions that begin with "Is?" and "Are?" and concentrate upon probing questions which can always be pursued with a "Why?" The question has always been an important teaching tool to stimulate the teaching-learning activity. In general, questions can be either categorized as restricted thinking questions or as expanded thinking questions. The restricted thinking questions call for factual knowledge, accepted answers, or facts previously learned. Responses to questions of this nature belong to the lower level of the cognitive domain, whereas responses to the expanded thinking questions come from the higher levels of the cognitive domain. The expanded thinking questions result in open-ended responses, the application of principles and the solutions to problems. In teaching religion both types of questions are employed; however, in order to assist the learners to value their responses and to stimulate and generate thinking, the teacher should make a conscious effort to structure expanded thinking questions within the activity of the teaching-learning situation.

Asking questions properly and generating thinking is an important skill if used correctly. However, the teacher must follow through by listening attentively to the response and really hearing what is said. This is more difficult than would appear at first glance. It is sometimes easier to put persons into a "cubby-hole" from which we expect to get, and usually do (or think we do) get certain behavioral responses. One example of this is categorizing: "All Irish-Catholics think that . . ." and concluding that because a learner is Irish-Catholic he thinks. . . . Another is labeling, namely, "He is an 'upstart,'" therefore, all the learner's behavior is upstart behavior. Still another is evaluating, namely, "This class would never appreciate this technique," therefore, I will not try a creative approach. It is this latter thinking probably more than any other factor which contributes to lack-luster teaching-learning experiences in religious instruction, especially if it is on a once-a-week basis. In short, what the learner says to the teacher comes to teacher through the teacher's own perceptual screen. Because responses are also filtered through the learner's affective state, it is well to stop frequently to paraphrase back to the learner what you have heard and wait for affirmation. Or, better, still, ask the learner to tell you what you have said. Do not assume that the person listening to you is really hearing you.

As stated above, the learner's affective domain is a vital reality in the teaching-learning situation. In the interaction of the religion class, as elsewhere, feelings are being expressed. Words are the least important part of any conversation. If the feelings are not identified and acknowledged, then word content is lost. It is the ability to do this that spells the difference in teacher effectiveness. In a sense the more "human" the teacher is, the more able to empathize with the learner, the less he/she is "teacher" in the commonly held concept of the role of teacher. He/she is no longer the dispenser of words of wisdom, the absolute controller of the learning situation. He/she is, instead, a sharer in a mutual growth experience. If there is not mutual growth, then one would question whether or not learning has occurred. There is no question that affective teaching-learning requires more of the teacher than a strictly cognitive approach. It necessitates that the teacher be accepting of him/herself, sensitive to his/her own affective needs and be willing to share this with the learner. As Gregory states, "It asks you to be fully human by not being a "teacher." Coping with affect requires you to *act* when the natural response is to *react*. Using affect as content implies that you can be mindful of the consequences of your actions. Affective approaches require that you can be secure enough in your own humanity to lay your humanness on the line when it is most threatening."[12]

Storytelling incorporates the skills of questioning, listening, and responding within the activity of a teaching model for the purpose of assisting the learner to reach a specific goal. Telling an account of events in an interesting and vivacious manner is an art ever old and ever new. Storytelling is in a sense an audio-visual production in that it includes the use of sounds, the painting of word pictures and the expression of feelings. Effective storytelling does not moralize and yet it generates questions and thinking by the listener. An example of this type of storytelling is found in the story of the Good Samaritan (Lk 10:25–37). In this story Jesus responds to the needs of his listeners by answering the question, Who is my neighbor? interwoven in the fabric of the story is a picture of a man left half-dead by the road and Jesus skillfully shows the feelings of the characters involved in this scene. Finally, Jesus puts a question to his listeners to respond to from their own feelings. If the teacher is not comfortable in this, an alternative is to have someone who is paint the word picture that develops characters with feeling, and record these images on a tape recorder.

Audio-visual materials can also be a valuable tool for the teacher of religion if they are incorporated into a teaching model. Media is the message has become a standard McLuhan phrase. Yet, oftentimes, the media is employed in such a manner that it is dissociated from the message. While it is true that good media has its own message, it is also true that media, i.e., a filmstrip, used to entertain, to fill up time, and so forth, has little measurable impact in the direction of the desired outcome or goal. Media must be selected with the goal in mind if it is to be effective. It must be selected with a view to the climate if it is to be affective.

The use of audio-visuals, which includes filmstrips, movies, slides, tapes, recordings, is highly encouraged. Since many/most religious education classes are scheduled after school or on Saturday morning, the teacher, in a very real sense, faces a dual problem. First, the learner comes to the religious education situation from learning experiences which are heavily saturated with A-V materials; if the learning experience offers too great a contrast, the learner is "tuned out." Second, the learner who comes enthusiastically to religious education class, eager for the message, is a rare commodity. It is, therefore a challenge to the teacher to make the learning experience a place where the learner really wants to be.

While stress has been placed on the use of A-V per se, it should be remembered that these are only one aspect of the multimedia, multisensual approach to learning. In proportion to the teacher's abilities to use them effectively, art, drama, and music are effective techniques for generating learner involvement.

The Cove model is proposed with religious educators in mind—not only for those who are involved in teaching in the traditional CCD model, but also for those who are in leadership positions who must establish the direction for a total parish program. For the former, who may not have the specific educational background for their work, it should provide a unifying thread which will tie together much of what they have been doing. For the latter, it will expand the vision of what can be done. It would seem that, unless these efforts are rooted in educational theory, concretized in a teaching/learning model, much goodwill and a great deal of energy will have been expended with little measurable effect on the faith community.

Questions for Discussion

1. Why is it necessary that the thrust of the religious education program be future-oriented?
2. How could a deliberate attempt to incorporate the four C's discussed in this chapter improve the quality of a parish religious education program?
3. Much has been said about the importance of shaping the climate. How would you go about shaping the climate for an effective parish religious education program?
4. It is often assumed that a committed Christian is an effective religious educator. Point out the fallacies of this assumption.
5. Why is it important to have the learner involved in establishing goals, selecting activity and structuring the climate in a religious education experience?
6. The key to any good teacher-learner experience is effective communication. What might be done on a parish level as a practical way of improving communication skills?
7. The Cove model was introduced specifically for religious education programs. Why is it important to operate out of a model?
8. We have often concentrated our efforts in teaching religion on content. What effect would a conscious concentration on teaching for Christian living outcomes have upon your parish program?

III

Teacher Development: An In-Service Program for Teachers

One of the most critical problems facing the parish director and/or coordinator of religious education is the need to develop a stable staff who are not only people of goodwill but who are also competent to teach the gospel message. A survey of the past five years of the teaching staff of the religious education program of almost any given parish will usually indicate that while there is a core of people who have been with the program for a few years, there is, nevertheless, a rather high turnover of teachers. This situation in itself leads to inconsistency and confusion. While undoubtedly there are many reasons why this is so, it is more than likely that the prime factor is a feeling of inadequacy either in teaching doctrine or in relating to learners.

Many directors have sought the solution to this dilemma by encouraging teachers to attend workshops on the deanery, diocesan, or regional levels. These are valuable and good, primarily because of their motivational value, but they often do not meet the need at the local level. Some directors have initiated local workshops; for example, teachers meet once a month to prepare as a group for the next three or four sessions. These, too, are valuable and good, primarily because of their support value. However, the question arises as to whether or not either system increases the competencies of the individual teacher. There is no doubt that the teacher grows in confidence in the natural give and take of the latter situation insofar as the emphasis is on the "how to." There is considerable doubt as to whether or not it develops the wider good which is, or should be, to assist the teacher in understanding, relating, and sharing the threefold dimension of the gospel message, that is message, community, and service. Because the situation differs from parish to parish, it is difficult to make specific proposals for the "how" and "when" of a teacher development program that is competency based and rooted in theory. Having experienced several time schedules for a program, we strongly recommend that a minimum of twenty teaching-learning hours be set aside in a concentrated span of time, for example, two consecutive weekends, or one or two two-hour sessions weekly. This concentrated time is needed to effectively communicate the philosophy of the program, to establish group goals, to teach skills, to develop the competencies upon which the teacher development program is based. The Cove model which is pivotal to our program should be applied, at least in theory, to specific teaching-learning situations within the parish whether they relate to children, parents, the elderly, or other adults. Moreover, it is necessary that the staff, whose energies are to be spent in creating the warm and loving climate of a faith community, experience community among their peers, and this cannot be accomplished in a less concentrated time-effort. Assuming that the recommended time schedule can be arranged, we present an overview of the ten two-hour sessions which were developed as Phase I of our teacher development program. This program was presented to groups of thirty to forty teachers who already shared two common interests. First, for the most part they came from parishes located within the same civic community, and second, they were already involved in the religious education programs of their parishes. Hence, there were already some common expectations from the course.

Assessment of Needs

It is imperative that facilitators of learning (workshop leaders) share their goals and expectations with the participants. Conversely, it is equally imperative that participants share their goals and expectations. Unless this is done, it is quite possible for the facilitator to come in with a prepackaged program which really does not address itself to the needs of the participants. Hearing the expectations of the participants at the outset, one can tailor the program to meet particular needs and to define realistic goals. Moreover, this enables the participants to experience that the learner can effect the teaching-learning situation—a fact which will be reinforced as the Cove model is presented and developed. Moreover, sharing goals, expectations, and needs assessment at the outset provides a built-in means for evaluation of the program.

Establishing clearly defined goals also helps to keep the group within the parameters of their expressed areas of concern and can be used as a check-list in terms of accomplishment and/or accountability at any point in time. Once the group has defined its goals and, if need be, prioritized them, they have in a sense entered into a contract. If this contract is not being kept because the facilitator is straying from the predetermined course, then it is up to the participants to call the leader to accountability. If this contract is not being kept because the participants are not lending themselves fully to the experience, then it is up to the facilitator to call them to accountability. The important point to be grasped from the assessment of needs is that participants experience and appreciate that, as learners in the in-service workshop, they have an active share in shaping the teaching-learning situation. Furthermore, it provides the participants with a working model of accountability and demonstrates how this can be applied to their parish program of religious education.

Approaches

In the initial assessment of needs session, the facilitator is the catalyst who more or less determines a very important dynamic. That is, will the group through the interactive process solve its problems, or will the facilitator function as the dispenser of all wisdom and knowledge, fielding questions from every source and providing answers? Establishing the climate in which the group feels free enough to solve its own problems demonstrates that learning is not a back and forth process between teacher and learner but that effective learning occurs when learner interacts with learner. This can be an entirely new experience for adults, particularly those who have been programmed to listen to the teacher (a priest, minister, doctor, professor, etc.) and to respond only to the teacher or to make no response at all. Diagragramatically the teaching-learning situation was as follows:

$$T \longrightarrow L_5$$

$$L_1 \qquad L_4$$

$$L_2 \qquad L_3$$

One of the problems with this model is demonstrated by L_5 who has effectively shut off the teacher. How is the teacher to know that L_5 has blocked out all communication? If the workshop facilitator (T) is really concerned with the importance and dignity of each person and is fully convinced that each participant has something to contribute, then diagramatically the teaching-learning situation is as follows:

Being less tied up on "one way" streets, the T in this situation is freed to observe that L_2 is a nonparticipant and can take the initiative to involve the learner in the group. This is not to imply that the nontalker equals a nonparticipant. Oftentimes nontalkers make excellent summarizers who, at the end of the discussion, briefly tell the group what has been heard. If the group is a subdivision of a larger group, then the summarizer's role becomes more important when called upon to report what has occurred in the subgroup.

The facilitator (T) of the workshop must take care not to be caught up in the dynamics of the group activity. The facilitator provides leadership in shaping the climate, assessing the needs and keeps things moving in the direction of the goals. If that role is relinquished, then the probability of success has been considerably decreased.

Performance Objectives

In order to teach for learning and living outcomes it is helpful that the teacher keep specific objectives in mind for each aspect of a given teaching-learning experience. It is to be noted that in the model the goal is introduced—representing an overall concern for the teaching-learning experience; however, the performance objectives are seen as specifics to carry out the broader dimension of the goal. These objectives are referred to as performance objectives since they are expressed in a form of "doing." They also provide a criterion for evaluation when expressed in this manner. By using performance objectives teachers can take much of the guesswork out of teaching. Through the correct use of performance objectives we can remove the "fuzzies" from the teaching of religion. Teachers are often heard saying, "What do I want to teach today?" or "What am I going to teach today?" This does not provide a sound basis for learning. The question to be answered in terms of learning outcomes is "What do I want the learners to learn?" Objectives should always be stated in terms of learning outcomes, and for teachers of religion we should go a step further and state objectives in terms of Christian living outcomes. it provides the teachers with a direction which they can share with others; second, it provides a guide for selecting instructional matter and methods; and third, it provides a guide for evaluating the learners.[1] The first question, "What do I want the learners to learn?" is followed by a second, "How can I prove that the learners learned it?" Performance objectives require that teachers state objectives in terms of expected learning outcomes and behaviors. Each objective begins with a verb and there should be only one general learning outcome for each objective. Because objectives are written in this form, performance can be measured and the teaching-learning situation can be evaluated.

Using the *Taxonomy of Educational Objectives: Cognitive Domain* edited by Benjamin S. Bloom, the table on pages 59–60 was developed specifically to assist teachers of religion in an in-service program.[2]

Once teachers are familiar with the cognitive domain and can differentiate between the lower and higher levels, performance objectives using both levels can be developed within the teaching-learning experience. This provides teachers with an effective tool to get away from simply teaching for knowledge and comprehension and helps them to incorporate the higher levels of the cognitive domain; namely, analysis, synthesis, and evaluation. Higher levels, of course, can be used effectively, only when the learners' cognitive development is sufficient to warrant their use. The catechism, with the familiar question and answer format, was geared to the lower levels of development. For many years we assumed that the learners' ability to regurgitate predetermined answers to predetermined questions was a reflection of acceptance of Christian living values. Unfortunately, and perhaps even tragically, this was not so. Unless the learner is capable of analyzing, synthesizing, and evaluating the product-content, it never becomes part of a value system. In the instance of a program for younger learners, the teacher should be alert for cues that the child has reached the stage at which higher level performance objectives can be effective and use them. Thus, the religion teacher is able to incorporate the principles of teaching and learning theories in producing Christian living outcomes.

In all teaching experiences, but especially in teaching

COGNITIVE

LOWER LEVELS

KNOWLEDGE

Brief concept, facts, rules

HOW TO STATE?

In terms of *doing:* e.g., define, identify, names, selects, states

Examples:
1. to name the seven sacraments
2. to select water as a sign of baptism
3. to identify Moses

COMPREHENSION

Understands the meaning of material—facts and principles

HOW TO STATE?

In terms of *doing;* e.g., words, explain, give examples

Examples:
1. to give three examples of how one can practice the beatitudes
2. to explain the meaning of covenant
3. to give in own words the parable of Good Samaritan

APPLICATION

The ability to use learned materials in new situations. Application of rules, concepts, principles and laws

HOW TO STATE?

In terms of *doing;* e.g., relates, shows, demonstrates

Examples:
1. to relate how having a fist fight on the playground violates the fifth commandment
2. to show a modern version of parable of Good Samaritan
3. to demonstrate with posters the relationship between creation and ecology

continued

COGNITIVE, continued

HIGHER LEVELS

ANALYSIS   *HOW TO STATE?*

To break down material   In terms of *doing;* e.g.,
into parts as related to the   identify, compare, contrast,
whole; to distinguish similar-   analyze
ities and differences

Examples: 1. to contrast qualities of Joseph to his brothers
           2. to compare Joseph (Old Testament) and Jesus
              (New Testament)
           3. to analyze ten commandments and Jesus' New
              Law of love

SYNTHESIS   *HOW TO STATE?*

Rearrange parts into a   In terms of *doing;* e.g.,
whole with emphasis on for-   writes, tells, summarizes
mation of *new* patterns

Examples: 1. to formulate a code of behavior for classroom
           2. to write a prayer on respect for God's creation
           3. to summarize a modern parable on sin and
              reconciliation

EVALUATION (Highest level)   *HOW TO STATE?*

Judgments based on evi-   In terms of *doing;* e.g.,
dence (either internal or ex-   judges, explains, concludes
ternal criteria)

Examples: 1. to explain why a society to be healthy practices
              the beatitudes
           2. to conclude that confirmation is the sacrament
              of adult commitment
           3. to judge that society has a responsibility for
              sick, aged, orphaned, etc.

religion, there is a need to teach the whole person. This means being aware not only of cognitive learning but also of affective learning. A guide has been developed for affective learning called *Taxonomy of Educational Objectives, Handbook II: Affective Domain* by the authors Krathwohl, Bloom, and Masia.[3] This handbook is an important tool as it develops the affective domain on levels similar to the cognitive domain. It is particularly necessary for religion teachers to be aware of the affective domain in order to teach for values and attitudes. Teaching for affective outcomes needs to be done as consciously and as specifically as teaching for cognitive outcomes. It is a mistake to assume that in teaching for cognitive learning the affective outcomes will be automatic. Teachers of religion should state performance objectives which will include the affective domain.

The following is the taxonomy of education objectives for the affective domain.

1. *Receiving*

This level refers to the learner's sensitivity to the existence of certain phenomena. This category consists of three areas: awareness, willingness to receive, and selected attention to phenomena.

2. *Responding*

At this level, the learner is sufficiently motivated and is actively attending to phenomena. This category of responding is reflected by the learner's demonstrating a willingness to comply with regulations, a willingness to respond, and a satisfaction in responding.

3. *Valuing*

The learner displays certain behaviors with sufficient consistency to reflect a general attitude. This category is further expressed by the learner's acceptance of a value, preference for a value, and a display of commitment or conviction.

4. *Organization*
   The learner internalizes a value system and demonstrates the ability to select values and to organize values into a coherent system.
5. *Characterization by a Value or Value Complex*
   The learner has internalized his/her values to such an extent that this value system becomes a way of life.

It is, therefore, crucial that in teaching for a faith response and Christian living outcomes that teachers employ affective performance objectives as well as cognitive objectives. Certainly, by using the suggested infinitives found in the handbook and following the procedures for writing performance objectives, facilitators of in-service teacher education programs can assist teachers to become aware of this most important aspect of teaching affective learning outcomes. This is one concrete vehicle for assisting the learners with their faith development.

Performance objectives are road maps for teachers and provide the direction for the instructional dimension of the teaching-learning experience. However, before selecting objectives there are specific considerations to be noted. The following was designed for an in-service teacher program.[4]

Considerations in Selecting Objectives

1. Are the objectives directly related to the lesson?
2. Are the objectives helping to develop Christian living?
3. In selecting objectives, am I aware of the background of the learner? (Abilities and past experiences) Examples: Are they used to working in a group? Are they familiar with bible services? What is their past experience in using the church?
4. Are teachers aware of what other levels are teaching and

doing? Is there maximum cooperation among all involved in the religious education program? (Teachers, parish coordinators, principals, priests, parents)
5. Are the objectives in harmony with the following principles of learning:

    1. *Readiness*—Do they have the necessary experience, maturity, and educational background to proceed successfully?
    2. *Motivation*—Is material related to their interest? Learners grasp what is meaningful to them.
    3. *Retention*—Do the performance objectives reflect learning outcomes that tend to be retained longest?
       Retention—through reading alone 10%
               —through hearing alone 20%
               —through hearing and seeing 50%
               —through hearing, seeing, speaking 75%
               —through hearing, seeing, speaking, doing 90%
    Therefore, we should teach for understanding and application (vs. rote) with emphasis on activities (doing) related to objectives.
    4. *Transfer*—Learner applies what is learned to other situations. Examples: arithmetic and grocery store; commandments and behavior in life situation.

With these considerations in mind, teachers are better prepared to select or write performance objectives that are consistent with learner's abilities and the realities of parish life. Teachers of religion are reminded again that there is only one objective for one learning outcome. The objectives become a guide for teachers to employ in developing and sequencing what the learners are to master within a given session. If the learners can accomplish the objectives, then the teacher can move on to new objectives, and if the learners fail to accomplish the specific objectives, then the teacher must reassess the objectives in light of the *Considerations in Selecting Objectives*. It is precisely this to which we referred as shaping the climate in the discussion of the Cove model. Again, it is the teacher's skill in assessing the situation and his/her flexibility in adjusting to meet the needs of the learner which will determine whether performance objectives will be achieved. Using performance objectives gives teachers a means for evaluating their teaching as well as the learners' abilities to master the objectives. Through this system of feedback the "fuzzies" can be removed from the teaching of religion and the opportunity for teaching for gospel values can be realized. It is a consistent approach rather than a hit and miss approach. It is important to note that the majority of textbooks mention objectives and goals; however, few teacher's manuals state objectives in terms of the learner, write them in hazy terms, and they are seldom stated in relationship to performance. Most teacher's manuals state their objectives in relationship to what the teacher is to teach rather than in what the learners are to learn. Furthermore, these objectives for performance are written in vague terminology and are of little assistance to teachers. Mindful of this, facilitators of in-service programs for teachers should stress performance objectives so that teachers may rewrite the objectives in the manual in terms of the learner's performance. Once the concept of performance objectives is grasped by the teachers then the other components for effective teaching and learning seem to fall into place.

Learner

The most important factor in any teaching-learning experience is the learner and the model emphasizes this point. Unless the teacher is aware of the learner and sensitive to where the learner is in most aspects of his/her development, many cues essential to the shaping of the climate can be missed or misinterpreted. This does not mean that the teacher needs to be a qualified psychologist, but it would be extremely helpful if an in-service workshop provided at least an overview of the major developmental theorists and that personality, cognitive, and religious development be considered.[5] Granted that in-depth study of these areas would be beyond the possibilities of a given workshop situation, enough should be introduced that the teacher is aware of the normal behavior patterns of the average learner.

In regard to personality development, it would be well to point out that in any group there will be a range of levels in development. Recognizing behavior as level-appropriate, even though not age-appropriate, will do much to relieve teacher anxiety. For example, if in a group of eighth graders there is, as there usually is, a learner who psychologically is in the third grade, it is level-appropriate for him/her to want to be up and doing (activity oriented) even though it is age-appropriate to assume a less active role. The uninformed teacher can interpret this as the mischievous youngster trying to stir things up, or worse still, can conclude that the total learning experience is a failure. In either circumstance, teacher tension is aroused and teacher effectiveness is adversely effected. If the teacher is informed and is functioning out of the model, the climate can be reshaped to meet the need of the individual learner while, at the same time, working toward the goal which had been established for the larger group. Knowing that the learner will be part of the group for a period of time, for example, a semester, also enables the teacher to write both specific and long-range performance objectives which will assist the learner to teach the goal of the teaching-learning experience.

As with personality development, any group will consist

of learners on different levels of cognitive development.[6] Certainly, enough basic theory should be introduced that the teacher is made aware of the intellectual capabilities of a learner at a given level. Two factors enter into this consideration. First, the natural intellectual endowment of the learner and second, the life experiences which have affected the learner's ability to grow to full potential. Familiarity with theories of cognitive development enables the teacher to write performance objectives consistent with the mean cognitive level of the group. For those learners whose development deviates significantly from the group mean, performance objectives which address individual needs will have to be developed. This is important because if performance objectives are not geared to the cognitive level of the group and to the individuals who comprise it, no amount of effort in reshaping the climate will lead to a successful teaching-learning experience. If performance objectives are too far below the cognitive level of the learners, the learners are bored. If performance objectives are too far above the cognitive and affective levels of the learners, the learners are lost. This does not leave room for the fallacious assumption that anyone ought to be able to learn religion by virtue of the fact that he/she had been baptized. It is unfortunate when to the waters of baptism are imputed skills most painstakingly developed by committed teachers.

Of equal importance is the faith development level of the learner. Perhaps it would be well to note that while we are treating these aspects of development as separate entities, we do so only as a matter of convenience, recognizing that all aspects of development are integrated in the total person. Faith development is also a major concern for religious educators. Since the learner of preschool and primary grade level is largely an affective being incapable of abstract thought and therefore incapable of truly grasping the concept of God, all efforts to foster his/her faith development must be addressed to the learner's affective self. As the learner grows psychologically and cognitively, more product-content can be introduced through the performance objectives. Again, in any given group there will be learners at different levels of faith development, but since the affective dimension should always be part of teaching-learning experience, it is perhaps somewhat easier to include affective dimensions which will reach the learner. Many of the texts from the major publishing companies include the faith development level in the suggested lesson plans, and it would be well to take note of this in preparing a teaching-learning experience.[7]

Activities

The adjustments to the developmental level of the learner, discussed above, will be made largely through the activity that will be used to achieve the objectives. As mentioned previously, the activity should always be consistent with the objectives and should be designed or selected to meet the needs of the learner. The model emphasizes the importance of flexibility in shaping the climate in the teaching-learning experience. This flexibility, except in unusual circumstances, should not apply to the objectives which are intended to give the teacher direction in planning the experience. Too great flexibility in the application of performance objectives would result in a one-way trip to nowhere. The activity, on the other hand, is to enhance the learner's involvement and to move the experience in the direction of the performance objectives. It is, therefore, recommended that two or three activities be planned, one geared to the mean developmental level of the group and in which the greater number will participate and two others geared to a higher level and to a lower level of development to involve those learners to whom they might appeal. In doing this, the activity, which is shaped by the performance objectives, flows with the teaching-learning experience.

It would be most helpful for the teacher to consult the worksheet "Considerations in Selecting Objectives" before selecting activities for the group. It is essential that the activity be consistent with these basic principles of learning: readiness, motivation, retention, and transfer. Just as certain activites are more suitable for learners on one level of development than on another; likewise, activities which motivate one group of learners, may not motivate another. Keeping in mind the psychological, cognitive, and faith development of the learner is an important consideration in selecting performance objectives. Another consideration in designing or selecting activities is to know the learners and their interests so that activities can be designed or selected to involve the learners in hearing, seeing, speaking, and doing to assure the most effective retention of desired learning outcomes. Finally, the activities shaped by the performance objectives should assist the learner to transfer learning outcomes into Christian living situations. Teachers can achieve most effective results by consistently applying these basic principles.

The importance of the developmental level of the learner and the specific performance objectives cannot be overemphasized in determining the activity for a group. If these factors are not considered, and considered carefully, there is a tendency to use the activity to fill a time-gap and, in this event, instead of enhancing the learning experience, the activity becomes a gimmick. The result is that both product-content and process-content are subverted. Conversely, when these factors are considered, the activity is a part of, and not apart from, the teaching-learning experience. Unfortunately, the misuse of the activity, possibly stemming from a misunderstanding of its function, has resulted in an attitude on the part of the learner that when the activity starts, the learning experience is over and the fun has begun. This attitude is found even among adults who have been exposed to this experience and who are reluctant to become involved in an activity on the adult level even when it can lead to a most effective learning experience.

In case there be any confusion it might be in order to clarify what we mean by activities. By activities are meant all processes that assist the learner to attain the desired learning outcomes. These processes include multi-media, art, liturgical services, field trips, role playing, drama and like processes. Used correctly, activities can help to achieve the stated performance objectives. Teachers should know why they have selected a specific activity, be familiar with the mechanical functioning of all hardware involved, and be comfortable in what they are doing. That a particular activity works well for one teacher and with one group is no guarantee that it will work well in another situation. If a film, filmstrip, or other media is planned, it should be previewed to determine its suitability and to measure its probable effectiveness. If the teacher sees the activity as a vehicle for moving in the direction of the performance objective and has had the time and foresight to make necessary preparations so that moving into the activity is a smooth transition into another phase of the teaching-learning experience, then the probability of a successful effort is rather high. On the other hand, deciding at the last minute to project a filmstrip one has never seen, using a projector with which one is not familiar, with a group of learners, can be an exercise in futility. Moreover, even if the necessary preparatory measures have been taken, teachers must be flexible enough to have an alternate activity if they realize that despite their effort the planned activity is not going well with the group. This may sound like a formidable task; however, as a rule of thumb for preparing activities: keep it simple, keep it meaningful, keep it consistent with the performance objectives.

Model

After the teachers had become familiar with the components discussed previously (the learner, performance objectives, and activities), the Cove model discussed in Chapter II was introduced. The model was not included until the components had been studied, as it was more meaningful to the teachers when they had a working knowledge of the theory upon which it is based and could appreciate the interrelationship among the variables. A further advantage of postponing the introduction of the model was that teachers could then more readily recognize their role as facilitators of learning. They tended to see themselves less burdened exclusively with the awesome responsibility to teach doctrine and more specifically charged with orchestrating all the variables into a meaningful teaching-learning experience. The model becomes dynamic when the teacher is able to interpret the visualization of the relationship between teacher and learner, between goal and activity, and among all the components of the model. When the teacher is able to adjust the variables so that the maximum needs of the learner are met, the probabilities are rather high that he/she is teaching for Christian living outcomes. Indeed, if the converse is true, one might reasonably question what has been accomplished.

While the main goal of Phase I was to lay the foundation for an effective teacher development program, it proved to be a community-building experience for participants who came to the realization of the key role they were playing in their local parishes. Moreover, they were able to apply the model to other aspects of their parish life. While the model was designed primarily as a visual reminder to teachers of their role as facilitators and to provide a consistent framework for planning and teaching religion in the formal religious education of the young, its application to adult programs, to parish councils, to any aspect of parish life is limitless.

Competency-Based Program for Teachers of Religion

However, in order to operationalize the model, the participants must develop the skills necessary to bring all the components together. The first, and probably the most important, is the ability to facilitate. The teacher as facilitator is emphasized throughout the program, and since it is a key element, there is a need to stress the concept of facilitator as a more dynamic role than is usually ascribed to the traditional understanding of teacher. Only when they see themselves as facilitators do participants fully accept the responsibility for shaping the climate. Workshop leaders teach this competency by allowing participants to share freely with each other throughout the workshop sessions. Once the importance of shaping the climate has been accepted, small group sessions on how to shape the climate are useful. The ideas gleaned from small group discussions are then shared with the total group. The talents and resources of the group surface, individuals realize they have much to contribute, and workshop leaders demonstrate what it means to facilitate. There is probably no better way to learn the value of sharing than by sharing. As participants become freer in this process and the workshop leader becomes part of the whole dynamic as a group member, participants become more sensitive to what is expected of them when they assume the teacher (T) role. If competency in facilitating is to be taught, it is important that the workshop leader participate in groups. If not, he/she is reverting to the traditional relationship of teacher to learner which is often one-directional. In this case, the workshop leader's experience and knowledge becomes a stumbling block to his/her own success.

Another important skill is knowing how to direct questions effectively. This skill was discussed in the chapter on teaching for learning. Participants found this competency most helpful in planning and carrying through their own teaching-learning experiences. An important part of questioning skills is the handling of responses. Responses, handled well, not only expand the thinking but respect the affective state of the learner. Since one usually asks a question to obtain information, it is quite easy to overlook the affective state of the person from whom the answer is elicited. Yet, this is frequently more important than the content of the response and to a great degree influences the teacher's ability to accept and appreciate it. Skill in this competency creates an atmosphere of openness and sharing. It encourages the learner to pose questions, assists in shaping the climate, helps in the assessment of teacher effectiveness, and is an index of the learner's grasp of the product-content.

Performance objectives are the basis for sequencing in that objectives provide a road map through the teaching-learning experience. There are three major factors that must be included when teaching for Christian living out-comes, namely, life experience, gospel message, and faith response. The life experience simply means that through questions, a story, or some similar procedure the teacher focuses the attention of the learners on the subject or product-content of the lesson. This is most effectively done by drawing out some actual experience the learner may have had. This should be done with the performance objectives in mind or it is possible that the life experience becomes the lesson. The gospel message, again with the performance objectives in mind, relates to the life experience, and the faith response follows as a natural consequence as the learners recognize the relevance of the gospel message to their daily living experiences. The faith response demonstrates that the learner has been able to interpret the life experience and the gospel message in such a way that he/she makes an option for Christian living outcomes. This will only result if the teacher has planned well, has clearly defined objectives, and can facilitate in the direction of the goal. The faith response is affective and can only be achieved to the extent that the teacher is able to weave the life experience, the gospel message, and the faith response into a meaningful whole. When this is done, the whole is indeed greater than the sum of its parts.

Participants need to be mindful, however, that they are dependent upon parental involvement in the religious education program. The learner's level of development is directly related to parental concern and parental values. This is illustrated in Chapter IV in regard to parent-child attitudes and beliefs in regard to death and afterlife. It is recommended that the goals and objectives of the program be shared with the parents and their cooperation be actively sought. While much of the success of the teaching-learning experience will be dependent upon teacher ability to facilitate the major components of the model, and to integrate the life experience, the gospel message and faith response, the incorporation of the faith response into Christian living outcomes cannot be sustained unless it is supported by the parents who are the primary educators of their children.

While all three components must be part of a religion teaching-learning experience, they do not each necessarily receive the same emphasis in time. Neither do they necessarily occur in the sequence mentioned. How much time is allotted for each component would depend upon the product-content, and, at times, the process-content of the lesson. If the learners are very young, or if the physical accommodations are not conducive to attention-giving behavior, the teacher might find it more effective to prepare shorter time periods for each and then repeat the process. The important thing is that all three be included in the teaching-learning process. Schematically, the relationship among these components is as follows:

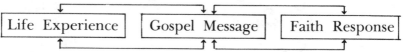

The emphasis that each component is given should be determined not only by the age, the circumstances under which the lesson is being taught, the developmental level of the learner, but also and always with the performance objectives in mind.

Sequencing for a teaching-learning experience basically

comes down to the teacher's ability to organize the product-content and process-content into time allotments which are practical. To illustrate, assuming a sixty-minute time allotment for the session:

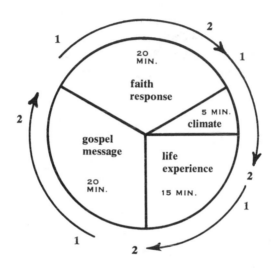

The diagram demonstrates a time schedule which should be flexible dependent upon the factors discussed, but should, at the same time, be applicable. If the teacher does not have some time reference, it is possible that one never accomplishes what one has planned. This will happen, on occasion, to even the most well-organized teacher. If it happens all the time, then the application of the product-content and process-content to Christian living will not occur. It is the application of the product-content to Christian living outcomes which determines the success or failure of the teaching-learning experience. This applies to the total program, not usually to the specific session. It would be very positive and supportive if, after any given session, teachers could observe more Christian behavior on the part of the learner. Yet, it seldom happens that way. However, at the end of a semester, or at the end of a program on the sacrament of penance, for example, changes in attitudes, values, and behaviors should be measurable.

These changes occur in somewhat the same way that a jigsaw puzzle or a mosaic is put together. The meaningful whole cannot be appreciated until each separate piece is put in place. If one has had experience with a puzzle or mosaic, or even observed either activity, there is a constant examination of pieces, trying and trying again to find the right piece for a given spot. This is analogous to what the teacher is doing when he/she evaluates a teaching-learning experience in light of the model, the three components of the lesson, and the performance objectives.

A competency based in-service program for teachers of religion offers teachers the opportunity to acquire specific skills and to enrich themselves as facilitators of learning. These skills help teachers to gain confidence in themselves and to work toward developing their competencies through careful self-evaluation.

Teaching Lab

Applying the principles and rationale for performance objectives, we asked ourselves, "What do we want the learners (in this case, teachers) to learn and how can we prove that they learned it?" We wanted them to learn the components discussed above and to develop the skills necessary to apply them in the context of the model. We felt that they could best prove they had done so by demonstrating it via a teaching lab. Therefore, teachers were asked to prepare a teaching-learning session which was video-taped and analyzed by the workshop facilitator and the group. In this instance, other participants played the role of learners. Other teachers elected to have the workshop facilitator visit them in the parish center during an actual experience with students. This, too, was followed by a discussion with the facilitator regarding the application of the model and the use of skills. Both approaches were effective and were in themselves a learning experience.

As the teaching labs were analyzed and discussed by the participants, several things began to surface, not the least of which was the realization that as teachers they shared many of the same concerns. Almost spontaneously a support community developed. More openness and, at times, lively debate ensued as to whether or not the demonstrating teacher had successfully used the model and the skills upon which it is predicated. This informal discussion and the labs enabled the workshop leaders to evaluate what, in fact, the participants had learned in Phase I.

Another important element which evolved from the teaching lab was a growing willingness of the participants to accept criticism from the facilitator and from their peers. Since most were functioning in their parish programs as volunteers with little or no formal training, they were unaware of the skills necessary for a successful teaching-learning experience. This awareness generated a willingness to continue with ongoing in-service education. Though the teaching lab may appear to be a contrived situation, it nevertheless provides an effective opportunity for personal evaluation, sharing concerns, and growth in confidence on the part of the participants.

Closing

At the close of the in-service workshop the leader introduced the assessment of needs that had been developed at
the first session, and participants were asked to evaluate the
effectiveness of the experience in light of the expressed
needs. This not only served as an evaluative process for the
group but also served as a vehicle of accountability for the
workshop leaders. Participants were asked to examine their
expressed needs before taking Phase I and to change or
prioritize them in view of their experience. This was done in
order that the program could be revised in areas that
needed to be strengthened and/or modified. Not unexpectedly, this evaluation resulted in requests for further programs in theology. Phases II, III, and IV had been designed
in anticipation of this need. Phase I was designed to meet
the needs of the volunteer teacher who lacked the professional background for teaching. Having been given some
insights into how to teach, we felt that teachers would then
be concerned with what to teach. It is certainly beyond our
expectation that the program will raise the expertise of the
parish programs to the professional level; it does, however,
provide the leaven for measurable improvement in the
quality of what is being done. Not to be minimized is the
support community which was formed in Phase I. One
might reasonably expect that were the model to be applied
to parish council and other aspects of parish life, then a
similar situation might be experienced. If so, then the
ground work for a faith community will have been laid and
more effective Christian living outcomes will result.

One of the pitfalls of a successful program is to sit back
and let it become static. We are aware that with the rapidly
changing values in our culture, we must be fluid enough to

meet the challenges ahead. We must continue to research for better ways to meet the needs of the faith community. We must evaluate the effectiveness of the traditional approach to religious education and be ready to move toward alternate structures. We must abandon the passive acceptance of societal mores and take the initiative in shaping the future. Certainly this will alter the role of the teacher as he/she becomes perhaps a neighborhood facilitator or a family religious education group leader. With the attacks on family life and family structure that bombard us on every side, it would certainly be appropriate to invest our energies in that direction. In any event, we must be prepared to provide creative leadership and dynamic support for those actively involved and concerned in this most important work of religious education.

Questions for Discussion

1. Why is the formation of a faith community among teachers and personnel (in a parish program of religious education) essential for a meaningful religious education program?
2. What is the value of a facilitator of an in-service teacher workshop operating consistently out of a sound teaching model?
3. What advantages are there for the facilitator of a teacher in-service workshop to be an active participant rather than assuming the traditional role of teacher?
4. Much attention has been given to performance objectives and the need to develop skill in writing them. Why

is it important that at least one affective performance objective be in every religious education experience?

5. Why is it important for the teacher to be aware of the various levels of the cognitive domain for an effective teacher-learner experience?

6. To what degree would familiarity with developmental personality levels affect teacher attitude toward the learner?

7. Why is it of value for teachers to facilitate activities to meet the learners on different levels of development? How could this be done?

8. In light of the high turnover of teachers, the decline in learner participation, the lack of adult involvement, what do you foresee as the advantages of a competency-based in-service teacher development program in your parish?

IV

The Theological Dimension of Religious Education

Successful religious education is rested in sound teaching theory. The daily or weekly sessions reflect such an integration of product-content and process-content that the two can be separated only on the logical level for analytical purposes. In the example used in Chapter II the product-content of the session could be described as the cognitive understanding of, the affective valuing of, and the disposition to practice charity. The process-content is the teaching-learning experiences in which the product-content is accomplished. This is to say that all the dimensions of the climate (commitment, consistency, cooperation, and communication), the teacher and the learner, the goal and the specific activities of the session are such that the product-content is the natural and expected outcome. This is not a claim for 100 percent success for each teaching-learning experience and/or religious education program. It is, however, a prediction that if success defined as the achievement of lifestyle objectives is constantly below expectations, one of several dimensions of the process-content are causing interference.

While it may be difficult to sort out the various dimensions of the process-content and to analyze their interaction in a given situation, the goal of successful religious education demands that this task be an ongoing one for all responsible for the religious education. This is true whether it is the religious education of a diocese, a parish, an adult organization, or a summer bible class. Each level requires the monitoring of the process-content in light of the expected product-content. Obviously, the smaller the group the more easily this analysis and any needed changes can be implemented. However, since larger divisions are composed of smaller units, a trained coordinator can encourage and lead those responsible for each group to regularly incorporate this analysis and correction into their understanding of their role.

Together product-content and process-content equal the teaching-learning experiences of religious education. Through the integration of the product-content and the process-content, religious instruction is experienced as a lived faith and the learner is better able to extend his learning into all the dimensions of his life. It is only when this is done that religious education achieves its goal of making faith a living faith. By a living faith is meant one that is informed, conscious and active in a religion which is integrating and liberating, both in one's personal life and in the life of the community.[1] This is an ambitious goal and can be achieved only over time and in accordance with the overall development of the persons involved. However, unless the religious instruction is perceived, planned, and executed to develop an integrated religion that is liberating, it is not contributing to the true religious education of those involved, even if they are increasing in knowledge about religion or in theological astuteness.

Both the product-content and the process-content are influenced by theology. Sometimes this influence is direct and articulated as when one is explaining the relationship of baptism and confirmation or when one is planning an experience to emphasize an individual's need to be concerned about each other. In these cases the theological understandings must be explained and the learner, in keeping with his/her developmental level, should be shown the various historical influences in our present theological perspectives. How, for example, in the course of history the twofold initiation rite became two sacraments, now administered years apart in most countries, can be comprehended on some level by all. Today's increasing concern with vanishing natural resources offers an opportunity to root the common bond of humanity in the mystery of the Trinity. In every session explicit theological learnings and everyday living experiences mutually enlighten each other if the teacher has thought out these relationships and is in tune with the everyday world of the learners in a given situation.

At other times the theological influence is indirect and operating as an underlying, though unexpressed, assumption. Often only a careful, beneath-the-surface type of analysis will reveal this latter type of influence. It can be discovered, for example, when the internal ordering of the components of a teaching-learning session are studied. Does the session place the emphasis on cognitive learning to the exclusion of affective content? Is the reference to lifestyle behavior merely tacked-on at the end or so future-oriented as to be easily forgotten? Are lesser matters put in proper perspective? For example, is the relation of Christ-church-sacraments-sacramentals clear, or do medals (perhaps for perfect attendance) seem as important as the incarnation? The indirect influence of theology can be seen when the teacher-learner interaction is reviewed in relation to the stated purposes of the religious education program. For example, is respect for the individual a consistent characteristic of teacher-learner interactions, or does teacher behavior, verbal or nonverbal, nullify the best prepared session?

Whether direct or indirect this influence of theology is important because it is one of the chief shapers of the components of the teaching-learning experiences. Religious instruction necessarily includes the articulation of religious faith in theological language and theologically shaped rituals. Failure of those involved in religious education to question the theological implications and ramifications of the product-content and, especially, of the process-content can, and often does, produce a gap which the learner cannot bridge. This gap is sometimes expressed as the failure of the learner to live what he supposedly has learned. More often, however, the real difficulty lies in the teacher's failure to have probed the dynamic between the religion being taught and the theology which shapes it.

Examining briefly the components of the process-content as discussed in Chapter II, one easily discovers the influence of theology. Both the teacher and the learner bring with them all their previously acquired theological convictions, their own perception of the Christian worldview. These for better or for worse, become a filter through which new experiences must pass. God as forgiving and merciful is not easily internalized if taught by an authoritarian person, whether this is a parent or a teacher, or if one's experiences with the sacrament of penance are traumatic.

Certainly there can be and often is a wide range of theological orientations even within a given religion or denomination. In a study using a wide variety of basic orthodox belief statements, Jeffrey Hadden found, somewhat unexpectedly, a wide discrepancy even within a single congregation of the conservative Lutheran Church in America.[2] It should come as no real surprise that within an organization with as diverse a membership as that of most major Christian denominations one would find theological orientations ranging from conservative-literalists through all shades of progressives or radical-antinomians. Therefore, the assumption of a uniform theological orientation among those in a given religious education program could be a blind spot leading to high frustration for those involved. This is not a plea for uniformity of theological orientation. It is rather a call for recognition of and respect for possible different theological orientations, especially among religious education program directors and teachers, between parents and teachers or between teachers and learners. Unless this possibility of differing theological orientations is aired, a program's chance of success is diminished.

While this dimunition can occur in several ways, it most often results in the loss of distinction between the shared foundation (faith) and aim (growth in Christian living) and the unshared dimension of theological orientation. Such a situation produces unnecessary anxieties and diverts energy from the task of religious education. Hence the right to follow diverse theological orientations while sharing a common faith and maintaining the same religious affiliation must be recognized and respected if religious living is to be, for all concerned, a truly personal commitment. The neglect of the highly personal nature of commitment and the individualized understanding of faith in the effort to maintain a oneness of faith or, in some cases, a premature acceptance, is probably at the root of many of the so-called crises of faith of late adolescent or adult years. It has been previously remarked that commitment on the part of the teacher is basic. While perhaps a higher degree of correspondence between an individual's lifestyle and the way of life as proclaimed by the gospel is necessary for the teacher, commitment is no less truly required for the learner. It is this presence of commitment, in keeping with the developmental level on the part of the learner, which distinguishes religious education from proselytizing or indoctrination. Religious education (growth in Christian lifestyle behaviors), proselytizing (conversion tactics) and indoctrination (efforts that ignore free will) each stem from different theological assumptions. Theologically, religious education assumes faith and usually previous formal or informal introduction to the practice of religion or the living of Christianity. Proselytizing assumes the need to bring the learner from unbelief to belief or from one form of the practice of religion to another form. Indoctrination can proceed from either of the above assumptions but is distinguished from either by its refusal to permit questioning or difference of opinion without engendering guilt and/or exclusion from the group.

A successful religious education program composed of fruitful teaching-learning experiences demands the explicit stating of the theological principles on which the contributory efforts are based. Only when this is done and clearly understood by all involved can the distinctions among religious education, proselytizing, and indoctrination discussed above be maintained and the true work of religious education be allowed to proceed.

This understanding can, perhaps, best be achieved in regularly conducted in-service workshops in which all levels of the religious education program work together to improve the total effort. Input regarding theological positions on which religious education efforts, past and present, have been built could provide information from which very fruitful discussions could flow. Such information could likewise be a background against which demonstrations could illustrate the approaches to teaching which various theological stances encourage.[3] In this way a variety of theological positions can be brought to light in a non-threatening way and new ways of looking at things, theologically speaking, can be introduced.

It is this understanding of the theological convictions underlying the religious education efforts that encourages consistency and, therefore, permits accountability. A clearly stated theology of religious education frees the religious educator to establish and maintain a program with lifestyle objectives. Likewise, it frees the teacher to structure the learning experience aimed at promoting growth in Christian living and the discovery of a Christian worldview. Finally, this explication of theological assumptions frees the learners from proselytizing and indoctrination efforts which ignore both human and Christian characteristics. Only when this freedom exists can religious education achieve its goal of the person liberated in Christ and committed to Christianity in all dimensions of his life.

As the General Catechetical Directory (II, 17) points out, religious instruction is one form of ministry of the word. As do the other ministries, so religious education aims at the building up of the church in a defined area so that the whole body might be stronger, more Christ-like. If everyone involved in Christian education were more conscious of the theology of the church as the body of Christ, it is likely that all types of religious education efforts would be valued for their contribution in building up this body. This is not to say that all efforts are of equal value, but, as St. Paul reminds us, one part of the body cannot say to another, "I have no need of you" (1 Cor 12:21–24). So, too, the religious educator, curriculum planner, teacher, pastor, and parish boards must work together in cooperation with each other and with parents, students, and the wider Christian community if religious education is to result in a more intense Christian lifestyle for both the communities and the individual members and if the Christian worldview is to become more pervasive. Diversity is healthy but for it to exist in the Christian community it must first be unearthed and confronted by those most involved in religious education, both on the diocessan and on the parish level.

The recognition of differing theological orientations, the understanding of commitment as applicable to both teacher and learners, and the conviction that religious education is a cooperative venture facilitate the communication, both verbally and nonverbally, of the gospel message of man's redemption in Jesus Christ, of his liberation from those things which impede his full development as a child of God, and of the Christian worldview.

It is this amazingly simple and yet, for those who believe, profoundly life-altering message which is the theological base upon which all Christian religious education is structured. To convey this message with all its ever-evolving implications is the raison d'etre of all religious education efforts. This is the goal of the ministry of the word expressed in its broadest terms. It is the motive for structuring a climate in which Christian growth can occur. It is the measure against which all efforts must be evaluated.

The ability to articulate a theological position, the appreciation of Christian art, or the regular observance of a religious practice can never be allowed to become more than aspects of Christian living. All efforts must be ordered to the facilitation of the single all pervasive corollary of man's relationship with God: "Be ye holy as the Lord your God is holy" (Lev 19:2; Mt 5:40; Lk 6:36). The divine action of our redemption in Jesus Christ has made possible the attainment of this ideal. Religious education's only purpose is the facilitation of this attainment. All efforts, especially those involved in the process-content must be consistently scrutinized that the *what* is done and the *how* it is done do not blur the Christian call to serve God in freedom and love. The production of amateur theologians or historians of religion, of expert bannermakers or arrangers of paraliturgical functions are all very tempting goals in light of their feasibility. Hence, the religious educator, curriculum planner, parish priest, and especially, teachers must be constantly on guard against the substitution of an enroute or specific objective for the only acceptable general goal of Christians known by their lifestyle.

As has been shown, the process-content of religious education reflects the theological orientations and assumptions of all involved in this ministry, particularly of those who are responsible for its direction. However, it is clear that while process-content has a theological dimension, process-content is not theology. This is likewise true regarding the product-content of religious education. While the product-content has an even more obvious theological dimension, this does not make the product-content to be theology any more than a mathematical dimension makes chemistry to be mathematics or a geographical dimension makes history or bible studies to be geography.

Particularly since the Middle Ages, theology has moved into the world of theory and, as such, has become subject to the canons of intellectual inquiry. This is true, though perhaps in a lesser degree, of the study of religion which is more often pursued from the perspective of history, sociology, and/or psychology than from the orientation of faith-commitment and community life. Religious education, while it is enriched by all of these pursuits, is aimed specifically at facilitating a style of living.

This distinction is clearly seen when one contrasts the goal of religious education with the goal of theology. The aim of religious education is a deepending of Christian lifestyle while the aim of theology is a growing understanding of faith and revelation. Even the most profound theologian needs to be nourished in a climate of commitment, consistency, cooperation, and communication in order to grow in those religious behaviors which describe a Christian lifestyle and reflect a Christian worldview. These nourishing activities which flow from clear and precise objectives and which are carried on in a climate characterized by commitment, consistency, and cooperation will communicate the gospel message and its inherent challenge to discipleship, Christian living. Without these nourishing activities, that is, teaching-learning experiences planned to enrich the personal and community dimensions of being a Christian, there is little hope that a Christian way of life is going to result. These nourishing activities take place informally in the home and this foundation is built upon systematically in formal religious education programs.

Simply stated, the product-content of religious education, whenever or wherever it occurs, is religious living. For the sake of analysis, this can be further delineated as that "confluence of the thoughts, emotions, desires, and overt actions of a person to form an integrated behavior pattern and lifestyle."[4] Gradually, through informal and formal religious education in which all concerned perceive the goal as consistent Christian behavior, the learner will have integrated his cognitive understanding of theology and religion and his affective valuing of religious commitment in such a manner that he is consistently disposed to practice charity, both inwardly and outwardly. He will be recognized by his living of the command of Jesus for those who would be his disciples: "Love one another as I have loved you" (Jn 15:12).

Moreover, if this lifestyle is to be Christian in its fullness, then its components must be shaped by the major dimensions of the Christian religion: scripture, doctrine and ritual. Here again, upon probing deeper, one finds theology. It is theology which guides the interpretation of scripture, though scripture remains the norm for theological development. It is the discipline of theology which promotes as it guards the formulation and application of doctrine as well as the organization of rites and ceremonies. Gregory Baum calls theology "an act of religion whereby religion transforms itself and finds within itself resources to deal with the problems posed by the culture."[5] Understanding theology as an act of religion can deepen one's appreciation of the dynamic between the two and the resulting effect on religious living. How, for example, a person understands the religious significance of baptism or confirmation will affect not only the seriousness with which one prepares for and participates in these rites but also the living out of this newly acquired status as a baptized or a confirmed Christian.

Just as it is unsound for a religious educator, a curriculum designer or a teacher to attempt to guide, plan, or conduct religious instruction without a thorough understanding of the theory and practice of the teaching-learning dynamics, so it is unrealistic and self-defeating for the religious educator, the curriculum writer, or the teacher to be without a thorough grounding in theology: biblical, doctrinal-moral, and liturgical. Again this does not mean that religious education directors, planners, and teachers become occupied with being or producing theologians or liturgists. Rather it is minimum insurance that the religion which is encountered and the life-style and worldview that are fostered in and by the religious education program are theologically sound.

Without a sound teaching model, religious education can become goalless activity, time-filling happenings. Without a thorough grounding in theology, religious education will search for a substitute foundation. Some will seek to make the adopted textbook the foundation of their religious education endeavors, giving it a prominence and a totality which no work deserves. Some will use the marketbasket approach, incorporating into their daily or weekly session a technique read in the latest issue of an educational journal or heard at a recent meeting. Others will rely on their own understanding of the relationship of faith, theology, and religion, often without the benefits of a recent updating. Perhaps the most detrimental are those who proceed to teach "what they were taught, as they were taught" on the erroneous conviction that religion and, therefore, religious education can never change. Thus, without a theological education which has been kept current, there is the strong probability of sanctifying the past, stultifying the present, and stifling the future. Since it is hardly an overstatement to characterize today's world as existentialist, notwithstanding recent trends of nostalgia, such an approach to religious instruction or such a perspective for religious education is, with rare exceptions, doomed from the outset.

On the other hand a thorough understanding of the theological dimension of religion deepens one's understanding of religion and religious living. Thus it becomes a powerful ally, performing a gyroscopic function, in setting the performance objectives and in structuring the learning activities. A sound teaching model and a solid theological foundation are an unbeatable combination in providing integration and stability for the religious education program, unit, or course, and in preventing the gimmick or the whim of the moment from charting the course of our efforts. Successful religious education is a unique activity in which process-content and product-content are fully integrated to achieve the goal of developing a Christian lifestyle, and in deepening a Christian worldview for all involved in the teaching-learning experience.

Religious education is not equal to instruction in scripture, in doctrine, in moral principles or in liturgy although each of these can and does occur within the total program. Nevertheless, none of these is the goal of religious education any more than the goal of chemistry is to learn to balance an equation nor the goal of foods education is to be able to measure ingredients accurately. This, however, is not to underplay the importance and absolute necessity of systematic instruction in scripture, doctrinal and moral theology, or liturgy. Scripture is our source and our norm and anyone with a well-rounded religious education should be able to handle scripture competently. Doctrinal development and the evolving theological expressions of our faith and moral principles must be understood and appreciated before they can be internalized and lived. Likewise, liturgical expressions of faith and theological understandings are more fully participated in and, therefore, presumably more nourishing to religious life when seen as related to rather than separate from faith and theology.

Specific instructional goals do not in any way take away from the fact that the overall goal of religious education, as has been emphasized, is growth in Christian lifestyle. One of the behaviors which characterize Christian living is forgiveness of offenses. To illustrate the influence of the theological dimension of religious education in the structuring of the teaching-learning situation, this need to be forgiving can serve as an example.

The planning of activities and selection of materials to increase the cognitive understanding, the affective valuing and the overt practice of forgiveness is enhanced by the multifacetedness which a sound theology brings. Biblical theology provides a continuous picture of God as forgiving. In the story of the Hebrews, God is revealed as slow to anger and rich in compassion, forgiving faults, transgressions, and sins (Ex 34:6-7). To enter into the Hebrew experience through scripture reading and reflection is to encounter this characteristic of God with considerable regularity. Sometimes it is seen in God's dealings with his people as in the Exodus story. At other times it is seen through the oracles of the prophets, for example, Hosea, or as modeled in one of the ancestors as read in the epiclike account of Joseph and his brothers. It is the lack of appreciation for this characteristic of God—while intellectually assenting to it—that makes Jonah the antiprophet that he is.

In the New Testament we learn more clearly of the forgiveness of God both by Jesus' preaching[6] and by his example, in the forgiveness of one of those crucified with him (Lk 23:39-43) and particularly in his postresurrection appearances to those who had been more concerned with themselves than with him in his hour of need.[7] In an even broader sense, this need to be forgiving stems from the command to be holy as the Lord our God is holy and is most certainly a prime embodiment of the injunction to treat one's neighbor as one would want oneself to be treated (Mt 7:12). A core petition of both the Lucan and the Matthean version of the Our Father is that of making our own forgiveness dependent upon our willingness to forgive those who have trespassed against us.

In doctrinal theology, especially concerning the sacraments, a reinforcement of this need to be forgiving is seen. It is an evident outgrowth of our baptismal adoption as children of a forgiving God and of our initiation into a forgiving church. Even more clearly it must be seen as the necessary condition for the sacrament of penance to have its reviving and strengthening effect on the religious life of the recipient. Without this theological qualification the teaching regarding sacramental efficacy could degenerate into magic. Above all, in the sacrament of the eucharist, the symbol and nourishment of our unity in Christ, the need to be forgiving is an absolute. This doctrinal point is further supported by the injunction in Matthew to forestall liturgical participation when forgiveness is needed from another until it is obtained (Mt 5:23–24).

These theological understandings are an integral part of the religious education process at all levels. They must not be presented only as reasons for one or another church regulation. Rather, they must be experienced by the learner in equivalent situations, real or vicariously structured by the teacher. Often student aid is needed, as, for example, when a teaching-learning experience could be created by an instance of nonsharing. If the group has not had a recent experience of this, the teacher and a learner or two could simulate the experience for the group. From the feelings this arouses, it is relatively easy to guide the group to understand the need for forgiveness if unity is to be preserved and before it can be nurtured. There is, likewise, the opportunity to share feelings regarding the difficulty of both asking and receiving forgiveness and to develop a further appreciation of what it means to be children of a God who is often revealed as merciful.

Many liturgical and paraliturgical activities assume the need of being forgiving as a Christian behavior. In each eucharistic celebration there is the recitation of the Our Father and often there is the exchange of peace. Special events such as communal penance service, the ceremony of the Advent wreath, the adoption of Lenten practices and the celebration of feastdays provide the opportunity for growth in the understanding, appreciation and practice of forgiveness. The probability that this growth will take place and that a truly liberating religious lifestyle and a Christian worldview will develop is dependent upon many factors. Certainly one of these factors is the sound theological education of those most responsible for the religious education program—a fact too often ignored in the urgency of recruiting personnel and even in the planning of in-service programs for teachers.

Successful religious education doesn't just happen. The process-content and the product-content must not only never be working in opposing directions, but also must be complementary aspects of one unified act. Both must, in all dimensions, be rooted in sound education theory and practice and in thorough and updated understanding of theological developments. This type of preparation frees the program from slavish adherence to a text or from spur-of-the-moment happenings. Most of all it frees all involved, but chiefly the teacher, to clearly understand the relationship of the overall goal of religious education and the specific objectives of a session or a series. It is this understanding which enables all dimensions of the climate, the teacher and the learner, the goal and the specific activities of each session to so interact that the hoped-for product-content is the natural outcome.

Questions for Discussion

1. Assume a religious education teacher is anxious to monitor the process-content of each session. Can you suggest (a) various approaches to do this and (b) some specific questions which could be asked of oneself at the conclusion of each session?
2. A goal of religious education is a religion that is liberating. How does this quality manifest itself in the six-year-old? the parent of six children? the sixty-six retiree?
3. Many equate theological astuteness and proper wording of an answer to religious education. How does this effect program planning?
4. How would you explain to an anxious-to-volunteer teacher that his/her lack of recent, formal education in theology makes the acceptance of his/her offer impossible. Would you make any exceptions?
5. Using the recurring controversy regarding communion in the hand or the ordination of women, show how the *same faith* can be expressed from a variety of theological orientations.
6. What are some of the signs that indoctrination rather than religious education is taking place? In what ways could an inservice program help prevent religious instruction sessions from being used for proselytizing or indoctrination?
7. Why is it contradictory to expect a religious education

director or teacher who cannot competently handle the bible to achieve the goal of religious education? Can an in-service program supply for this deficiency?

8. Sound religious education recognizes that religion is culture-bound yet highly personal. What is likely to happen when these assumptions encounter the belief of some that religion, and therefore religious education, is unchanging?

V

Accountability and the Parish Community

Accountability is one of those terms which somehow or other slips into the vernacular, is frequently written about and talked about but, somehow or other, is never clearly defined. In education it is both a source of delight and confusion. For administrators, it represents a new approach to the old nemesis, discipline. For teachers, it looms too often as a rather frightening way of checking on teacher effectiveness. It is a term which has been used and abused at the discretion of educators. One might, then, appropriately ask what accountability means as applied to religious education and what it means as applied specifically to a parish religious education program.

Simply put, it is the vehicle through which all members of the parish faith community are apprised of and involved in the program, and through which they are asked to assume responsibility for its content, its process, and its effectiveness. The concept that all members of the parish are called by virtue of their baptismal commitment to participate in the parish program is frequently lost in the concentration on the mechanics of drafting volunteer (and often unqualified) teachers, in selecting the text, and in arranging a convenient time schedule. If this is accomplished, then the parish usually assumes that religious education is taking place. Thus, year after year, band-aids are applied without really sensitizing adults, all adults in the parish, to the fact that they have a personal and shared responsibility for its success.

With this in mind, let us discuss accountability as it relates to the four C's of the Cove teaching model as explained in Chapter II. Indeed the commitment, consistency, cooperation, and communication discussed in the context of the model are essential elements insuring that accountability is built into the program. Only through the conscientious application of the model can the spirit of accountability permeate the parish community. The spirit of accountability is the power plant from which total parish involvement will be generated. The individual must have a sense of involvement in the parish and an intimate involvement in the faith community before he/she can seriously raise questions regarding the religious education program or, for that matter, anything else that is going on in the parish. To do so would be a futile, time-consuming exercise in frustration because of its lack of purposefulness. The spirit of accountability, the sense of involvement, and the commitment which flows from it must exist on the broader parish level before individuals in the parish (parents, teachers, priests) can with any degree of integrity be called upon to accept the challenge to be concerned in a more personal, individual way for the responsibility for the program. For this reason, commitment is the primary C (C_1) in the model.

Consistency (C_2) in the model refers to the need of the committed parishioner to be concerned with the philosophy of the parish religious education board, the parish council education committee or to whomever the responsibility for the program is delegated. He/she should be concerned enough to be part of the formulation of the philosophy, the definition of terms and its conveyance throughout the parish. Moreover, that concern must carry-over to interest in the procedure for translating that philosophy into concrete programs with realistic goals to the end that everyone, from the new-born to the elderly, is affected by the parish program in a real and meaningful way. It might be well to give pause to the program as it exists at the moment in any given parish. In some (hopefully, few) parishes, the responsibility for this program is relegated to the youngest associate pastor whether or not he has any natural and/or expressed interest in the project; worse still whether or not he has any real and/or apparent talent for the task.

Other parishes have initiated PEP (parent educator programs) with varying degrees of success. Others have experimented with adult discussion groups; again with varying degrees of success. However, unless these programs are synchronized with the written philosophy of the parish, they function in a vacuum and, sooner or later, lose their effectiveness. The heart of the matter is that a parish as a faith community must spell out its philosophy; must raise the consciousness of its members to what its philosophy means in practical terms; must set for itself meaningful goals which reflect its philosophy; and must set up programs to implement the goals in a realistic and practical way which will touch the lives of all its members. It is this concerted effort to implement the philosophy of the parish that we identify as consistency (C_2) in the model.

If the parish philosophy reflects concern for the ongoing religious education of its members, and proceeds to design programs to meet the needs of all levels of religious development among its people consistent with its philosophy, it must follow that cooperation (C_3) among the various phases of the general program is crucial. It is inconceivable that the PEP, parish school of religion, adult discussion groups, etc., merely coexist. If cooperation merely means that no two groups sign up for the kitchen on the same night, this is accommodation, not cooperation. Cooperation means taking time to sit down, to discuss and to evaluate where the given program is, and where it is going, in view of the general philosophy of the parish. Cooperation is a key element in accountability, for it is only when all phases of religious education are mutually cooperative that a program can be dynamic.

Sitting down to discuss is the fourth C (C_4) of the Cove model. It is the catalyst or agent for change. It is only through communication or interchange on a personal level that an account of or evaluation of any given program can be made. The free exchange of people who have made a personal commitment (C_1) to the faith community of the parish, who are concerned with consistency (C_2) between what it says it is all about and what it is doing, and who are willing to cooperate (C_3), creates the atmosphere in which meaningful questions can be asked, even when these questions involve risk; an atmosphere in which an honest evaluation can occur, in which one dares to say what one means (C_4), rather than what is expected, is the dynamic which actualizes practice in an effective parish program.

For the most part, one must concede that this is not where most parishes are functioning. On a practical level—and one might use this to determine where the parish is functioning—have you heard these or similar remarks:

Parent: "I don't know what goes on in CCD (religious education). My daughter doesn't even have a book."—or—"I don't know about this CCD. I've read my son's book—there isn't a bit of doctrine in it. He doesn't even know the holy days of obligation."

Teacher: "These kids are in the fifth grade and they don't even know that there is a church. They must have been playing games for four years."

Student: "Why go? It's a drag. Never learn anything anyway."

Pastor: "The CCD program is the associate pastor's responsibility. I've done my bit with that."

Associate Pastor: "I'm not an educator—what do I know about running a program—I suppose I have to take a crack at it."

How accurately do these and similar statements reflect your parish scene. On a scale of 0–10 any score below 5 means that you need to evaluate what you are doing in terms of what we have been called to do in religious education by Vatican II, the National Catechetical Directory, and the pastoral *To Teach As Jesus Did*. If you score above 5, you might well ask, "Accountability—who needs it?" The fact is that religious education needs it (even those who score 9.9) in order to stay alive, and all those in any way concerned about religious education need it in order to grow in Christian living.

The point being made is that the total faith community must be involved in religious education. The age of passing the buck is over. No longer can anyone sit back and say, "That's not my responsibility. I have charge of visiting the sick, the altar boys (persons)." But someone must be in charge, must have the responsibility for religious education on the parish level. Is it the responsibility of the parish religious education (CCD) board? If so, in many cases, between program and board there is a great abyss of nothingness meeting two nonentities. But who has the responsibility? The answer is found in the spirit of renewal found in Vatican II. The whole concept of shared responsibility challenges each concerned and committed member of the parish community to take an active role in shaping the goals of the parish community. Fortunately, there are the goals of the parish community. Fortunately, there are instances where shared responsibility is apparent, where there is more active participation and involvement among parishioners in the life of the parish. In developing the concept of shared responsibility it would be at least foolish, if not tragic, to overlook what has already been initiated and fail to make use of what has already been operationalized as the basis for further growth. For example, in many parish communities it is common to see extraordinary ministers of the eucharist and deacons sharing responsibility for the liturgical life of the parish. In some parishes, the spiritual life commission of the parish council takes an active role in planning the liturgy for Sunday and special parish celebrations. Parishes with well-designed sacramental programs are focusing more and more on the role of the parents and on parental responsibility in the preparation of the child for membership in the faith community and active participation in its sacramental life. Moreover, by incorporating the reception of the sacrament of baptism into the parish liturgy, emphasis is placed on the responsibility of the faith community in the Christian development of the baptized throughout his/her lifetime. Emphasis is deliberately placed on the sacrament not only as a personal encounter with Christ but also as having special meaning within the context of a faith community. A welcome and hopefully growing phenomenon is the presence of a professionally qualified parish coordinator of religious education (DRE). Parish coordinators share, or should share, in the leadership of the parish in a decision-making capacity, particularly as those decisions affect the total program of religious education.

A further example of sharing responsibility of the parish community is expressed in parish councils. In those instances where the parish council is viable, its members coordinate all aspects of parish life, from financial matters to spiritual concerns, and thus share in building the Kingdom of God in the parish community. It is neither the function of this chapter nor of the book to advocate active parish councils, although the authors agree that they are indeed an integral part of shared responsibility on the parish level. However, if they do exist, they should be functional; that is, they should not exist for the privilege of confirming a decision that has already been made (and, too often, executed). The parish belongs to the baptized members of the community in a special and unique way; and every important decision affects them in a special and unique way. Because of this, every parishioner should be actively concerned with the composition of the parish council and the philosophical backdrop against which it is operating. Again, this should be spelled out in the philosophy of the parish itself. Only in this active concern do parishioners become aware of their mutual shared responsibility. Accountability in this instance is already operative.

Mutual shared responsibility extends to the ministry of priesthood, if priesthood is understood in terms of its universality in which we individually participate by virtue of our commitment to the church through baptism and confirmation. If one truly accepts this concept with all of its implications for members of the parish faith community (and the parish priest accepts it also), then the responsibility of the religious education of the community is a collegial responsibility demanding accountability which is predicated upon a unique degree of communication among priests, parents, teachers, concerned parishioners, religious education boards, and parish councils. This may sound like the proverbial "pie in the sky." One can almost hear: "You don't know *our* parish!" "What's a parish council?" "Our only problem is getting enough teachers to cover the classes." "I don't know what's going on in our religious education program. I suppose we have one—seems to me there is a notice about it in the parish bulletin." This is, unfortunately, true in too many cases. One has the choice of living with the situation or of taking positive action to remedy it. It is not the pastor's sole responsibility. An emergence of leadership as concerned adults set out to determine what the parish is offering by way of total religious education, what goals have been defined in the area of concern, what programs have been designed to implement the goals, what the parish community is doing to effectively demonstrate its support, is the dynamic which is the basis for an effective program. If the response is one of positive action, leadership will emerge when concerned adults begin to ask pertinent questions as they set out to determine what religious education is all about.

Actually, whether or not leadership emerges is dependent upon the willingness of those presently involved in parish administration to encourage adults to ask questions and to assist them as they search for answers. It is important that the emphasis be placed on "searching for answers" rather than on having the answer. There is a tendency to focus upon the immediate problem, for example, getting enough teachers to "cover" classes and, once enough have been drafted, to rest comfortably until the next crisis arises. Again, this is the band-aid approach. In concentrating on winning the battle one often loses the war. In the ongoing questioning, probing, searching for answers one must be willing to risk that the faith community will become aware of problems it did not even know it had. The type of leadership required for this involves adults who can work with others to find a solution to ever-emerging questions through genuine coordination of efforts, cooperation, and communication.

It would seem to be an oversimplification to state that the primary objective of the leadership group is to identify the problem. For example, it is easy to say, "We know what the problem is; we have twenty-four classes and only eighteen teachers," and then to proceed to put social pressure on predetermined members of the parish. The teacher who is already working six hours a day, five days a week in the public school situation is an easy target. (She knows how to discipline these kids.) It is somewhat more difficult (and painful) to explore why members of the parish who are capable of participating in the program have not sufficiently identified with the faith community to voluntarily offer to serve; or to explore why members of the faith community are diffident about their ability to communicate the message of the gospel due to their personal lack of knowledge and/or conviction. It could very well be, and often is, that the plumber who works with "things" all week would be a much more effective communicator of the gospel message because he/she truly enjoys working with people.

Following through on a practical level, suppose the group identifies a need for continuity in planning the curriculum for the parish school of religion or the necessity for developing a meaningful adult education program. Where does it go from there? Ordinarily, one would seek out the group in the parish responsible for this area of concern, e.g., the education commission of the parish council or the parish executive board of religious education. Often, to the surprise of the searcher, there is no such thing as the parish council. Has one then identified another problem? One might suggest that the tendency here is to throw in the towel. "We'll never have a parish council here; the pastor is hopeless." The fact of the matter could be that he is helpless in the sense that cooperation among the parishioners has been nil in matters of administrative concerns. If concerned adults are willing to serve in this capacity, take positive action by communicating your availability. This could well be a great learning experience for all.

It sometimes happens to the surprise of the group that there is a group of people who formulate the religious education board. Then, either one of two realities may be present. First, the group may be operating as a "paper board." In other words, it is a list of names submitted to the bishop and/or diocesan office to satisfy requirements or to satisfy the pastor's need to operate effectively ineffective as sole proprietor of the parish and the answer to its every problem. (It is somewhat overwhelming to imagine the number of hats that one person must wear if this be the case, e.g., spiritual director, confessor, financier, accountant, realtor, educator, etc., etc.) Second, there may be a group functioning well as a religious education board but with little or no communication with parents, teachers and other board members.

In the first instance, where there is no parish council, be aware that professional help as to the "how" of setting up an

effective board is always available through diocesan resources. In the second instance, the board needs the
"know-how" in communicating and sharing the highlights
of the program with the parish community. Does this not
open up a whole new vista of involvement of members who
would not be interested in other aspects of the program? At
least in this case there is a functioning board in need, nevertheless, of renewal and new ideas to spark enthusiasm.

Who is responsible for initiating change? Are you saying,
"Not I, Lord"? It is one thing to say that accountability is the
shared responsibility of all members of the parish community. It is also a universally accepted axiom that everybody's
job is nobody's job. Group projects with no one in a clear
position of leadership somehow or other never seem to get
off the ground. Without minimizing the basic thrust that
accountability should be and is the basic concern of the
committed Christian, the point is made that in every area of
responsibility there must be a pivotal person/persons to
whom the rest of the group are accountable in a special way
and who, in turn, is accountable to the group. The pastor,
or the person to whom he has delegated the responsibility,
is the ultimate accountable person. If you are reading this
chapter, you may more than likely be *the* pivotal person or at
least *one* of the pivotal persons in your parish. The pivotal
person may be the parish religious education coordinator, a
professional person with expertise in the administration of
the religious education program; the president of the religious education board who may be lacking in professional
preparation required for effective leadership; the priest
director who in all too many cases has more good will than
expertise; the principal of the religious education program,
etc., etc. In no case can this pivotal person function in a
vacuum. He/she needs active participation from all con-

cerned adults in the parish. The primary responsibility of the pivotal person is to orchestrate all aspects of the parish program so there is a sense of direction and to provide the vehicle through which the parish members can evaluate from time to time where they are in terms of where they have been and where they hope to go. This cannot be accomplished in a year. If the parish ever reaches the point that it can sit back and very comfortably say, "We've done it!" it might add also, "We've had it!" because it has stopped asking questions and searching for answers. Questioning, searching, growing are signs of life whether one is talking about an individual or a parish faith community. If the symptoms are absent, death is present.

Leon Lessinger, often referred to as the father of accountability because he pioneered the concept in education, states that there are certain characteristics which must prevail if there is real accountability.[1] While Lessinger was concerned with the formal educational setting of school, the characteristics he suggests are applicable to the pivotal person/persons in the parish religious education program. His first characteristic is *stewardship*. That is, that the pivotal person, or group, must recognize that they are important to the parish and to its religious education program. This is something to which we might direct much of our concern. Even if one's background in psychology consists in reading Dear Abby or her counterpart in the local newspapers, one has already been convinced that we are what people around us have let us become. If the concentration of the parish board has been on filling slots, e.g., "We need a fourth grade teacher—one who can handle boys," then the person who agrees to help is a "slot filler," important only in the sense that we now have someone in with the fourth grade youngsters. But how important, except in terms of convenience, is that person in relation to the total parish effort in religious education. Would any warm body have done just as well? Question—is this a key to the frustration—the feeling of isolation of so many teachers and the cause of the high turnover of teachers in so many programs? Is the teacher given the text, the manual, and then left to his/her own devices? Isn't he/she important enough for the faith community to share with him/her and others the very real concerns he/she may be experiencing about the faith development of the children, the Christians in process, in his/her class. In short, caring and sharing is the heart of the matter. A fact, not to be overlooked in this regard, is that the teacher is assuming a role that is primarily a parental responsibility—a responsibility that cannot be abdicated in any sense any more than they can morally abdicate responsibility for the child's physical and emotional well-being. It is a mark of real faith community involvement when concerned adults are concerned about setting up the program and concerned with the quality of the program which facilitates parental fulfillment of this responsibility. The individual teacher is assisting the parents and the faith community, and in this has the right to expect active support from both.

The second characteristic is *celebration*. Celebration is akin to stewardship in that the religious education board and the teachers are well aware of the responsibility they have assumed, are sensitive to the importance of what they are doing not only for the students and their parents but also for the larger faith community and rejoice in the privilege of serving. This is a far cry from those persons of goodwill who agree reluctantly to serve because they "can't say no to Father." Question: How many potential leaders are "caught" when the pastor or his associate calls and says,

"Look, will *you* do *me* a favor? I'm really stuck for a fourth grade teacher"? Put on the level of a personal favor which one cannot graciously refuse, it would seem very difficult for the recipient of the request to work up to celebration.

The third characteristic is *listening*. Listening in the context in which we are using it means listening as a conductor listens to an orchestra. If one has had the experience of being present at the performance of a symphony orchestra, one cannot but be impressed as the conductor orchestrates the various sounds and quality of the numerous instruments to produce an harmonious whole. In the same way the accountable leader is alert to the needs of the parish members, sensitive to their feelings, aware of concerns of parents regarding the program, and knowledgeable about the overall goals and expectations of the faith community. As a result of this active listening the pivotal person is prepared to make recommendations concerning the program even when doing so may include taking risks. If recognized as such, then celebration discussed previously follows as a natural consequence. It is when a person is filling a slot that frustration exists and nonlistening results.

Finally, the accountable person is an *entrepreneur* who, for the benefit of all persons involved in the program, gathers resources, makes suggestions to appropriate persons or groups, dares to pose questions that lead to searching, organizing and gives the best of which he/she is capable for the faith development of the parish community.

What does this mean for the parish program of religious education, and one must always read with the question "What does this mean to our parish?" in mind, or one is always reading about some other people in some other parish out there. When the pastor and/or his associate calls to ask a person to assume a role in the parish program in

whatever capacity, he is asking him/her to become accountable in a special way to the faith community. It means more
than "Yes, I'll sit in on a few meetings." It means that one is
willing to assume a position of stewardship and to celebrate
doing so. It is more than accommodating the pastor/
associate pastor, for accepting a stewardship role has a
gospel significance. "Whatsoever you do to the least of my
brothers or sisters, that you do unto me" has unique meaning for the accountable Christian. On accepting a position
of stewardship one becomes a pivotal person. To be truly
effective this person must be keenly aware of his/her own
gifts and talents and be capable of recognizing the varied
talents within the parish community. Moreover, he/she
must be capable of tapping these talents effectively. Thus,
he/she is able to participate in the growth and development
of every person involved in the parish program. In other
words, he/she is willing to work, or as Lessinger so aptly
expresses it, he/she celebrates his/her role. It would seem
that only a person who recognizes his/her own gifts as well
as the gifts of others is capable of celebrating the privilege of
doing his/her part in the continuing growth of him/herself
and others.

On the local parish level, being a good listener is probably
the keystone of what accountability is all about. It is in
listening that the pivotal person can become aware of the
effectiveness, or lack of effectiveness, of the parish religious
education program. It is also through listening that he/she
becomes aware of the talents of people involved in the
program and is better prepared to make suggestions for
improving its quality. In making suggestions the pivotal
person shares with others what he/she has heard, and the
sharing itself may initiate or stimulate other creative
suggestions.

The pivotal person as entrepreneur in the overall program is the risk-taker. While every teacher and every board
member must be entrepreneurs on the level at which they
are functioning, the person in whom greatest responsibility
has been placed must be willing to confront, to question, to
probe, to request, to provide direction, and to create an
atmosphere for change when that seems appropriate. This
person must also be willing to do so even when the doing is
an unpopular stance. Moreover, exercising responsibility
must be done in such a way, that the very people being
confronted, questioned, probed, and directed recognize
that the pivotal person is acting out of real concern for a
program that will meet the needs of the faith community
and not from his/her personal whims. The entrepreneur is
a change agent willing to take risks in order to create a more
fruitful program.

The qualities referred to above are the qualities found in
"doers." The parish program needs people who "do" as well
as think and discuss. In the final analysis, if there is a need of
a fourth grade teacher, somebody has to "do" the task. No
amount of discussion by the religious education board
would remediate the situation. The religious education
board would better serve the parish if it is composed of
"doers," that is, people who will go one step beyond iden-
tifying, analyzing, and discussing. It must be composed of
people who will "do" something positive toward a solution.
If the board is made up of people who are serving out of a
sense of duty and have no real interest in the program of
religious education, it is more apt to act as a rubber stamp
for the pastor and may not always be working in the best
interest of the faith community.

How does the local parish begin to create an effective
religious education program? The first step, it would seem,

is to identify from among the faith community a few key people with the qualities described as basic for an accountable person. Secondly, these become the pivotal persons who will take the initiative to evaluate the present program and pinpoint its strengths as well as its weaknesses. The weaknesses, so they may be eliminated; the strengths, that they may be built into the new program. Thirdly, they move from the program itself to the broader parish problems. It might be well to reemphasize that this cannot and will not be accomplished in a couple of meetings, for a study may point up a lack of parental involvement, a problem in communication, a lack of concern for the elderly, the absence of a program for adolescents and a feeling of alienation among young adults. Any one, or even several, of these situations may exist in the parish. (If so, do not be discouraged; you have plenty of company.) If only one exists, the task is relatively easy. If several, it would be well for the group to prioritize them and to go about solving one at a time.

Once the problems have been identified and prioritized, the group then works on the ownership of the problem. For an example, let us use lack of communication among teachers. There are several possible reasons why. The teachers may not even know each other; their paths may never cross due to scheduling; the physical setting of the center may not be conducive to teachers meeting each other, especially if there is not a room for teachers to meet over a cup of coffee; the religious education board or principal does not provide an opportunity for teachers to meet socially, and so forth. There can be as many reasons why as there are local situations. But, in any event, who owns the problem? It may be that the religious education board is so involved in the mechanics of the program that they lack the broader perspective of the program as an essential element in the faith community; therefore, they are not concerned with, and, moreover, do not see it as their task to be concerned with, community building experiences for teachers. It may be that teachers feel they have an obligation to fulfill and they would just as soon do it and be about other things. It could be that in an effort to provide smaller classes for convenience, or for whatever reason, the schedule is such that the program is atomized. It may be teachers who have not kept apace with changes in the church, who have taught for thirty years and will die happy with the Baltimore Catechism in their hands. Thus one sees that for every problem identified, the group must also identify its ownership. Only when ownership is determined can solutions be proposed.

Regardless of who owns the problem, the pivotal group must include the owner(s) in its solution. Solutions are never reached in a vacuum and they are never truly operative unless there is consultation with all who experience the problem. Teachers, in this example, should be consulted for suggestions for discovering ways in which communication can be improved. A very real risk in this is that some teachers may not even be aware there is a communication problem because they have not "been in touch." The pivotal group might also come to the conclusion that they are not the ones, either individually or collectively, to seek the solution. In this event, they should seek out someone who is qualified, able, and willing to address it.

Assuming that the problem, its ownership, and the person who can facilitate a solution have been identified, we propose the following procedure. Let the solution evolve from meaningful discussion among concerned people (the teachers) and pivotal person(s). Set up realistic goals which the group feels it can achieve with a reasonable degree of facility. If the intent of the pivotal person(s) is to work toward some form of accountability, then the established goals must respond not only to an immediate problem but will also respond to future needs. The immediate problem used as an example here was teacher communication. The future need could well be teacher education rooted in a sound teaching theory. Whatever the goals may be for a specific parish, it is vital that the goals be attainable and within the competencies of the group. It takes time and energy to become aware of the talents latent in the parish community which can be available as the parish moves to become a real faith community.

Let us now reflect on the steps discussed above in the context of the Cove model. First, one must focus on the learner (L), and in the parish community with an effective religious education program every parishioner is a learner, especially the adult who is concerned about his/her own religious development and is integrating this concern with his/her religious experience. We focus upon the teachers (T) with the communication problem as an example to explain the model in operation. The pivotal person(s) who is working with the group is the (T) in the model. The back and forthness between teacher (T) and learners (L) is the discussion which leads to identification, ownership, and solution of the problem. Goals set up of necessity must be practicable, attainable and within the competencies of the T and L as they work together. The activity (A) of the model is the vehicle which will be used to implement the goal, e.g., social programs to increase teacher communications. This does not imply that once an activity has been set in motion that the task is completed. The T and the L must constantly evaluate the A to determine whether or not it is effectively leading to the attainment of the goal (G). Accountability exists when both T and L are actively and mutually involved in the evaluation of the activity. The activity (A) which is designed without concern for the T, the L, and which does not move in the direction of the G is a prime example of the hit and miss approach which accomplishes little or no good, and that only by chance. To avoid this it is necessary to study the climate (C) in which the activity is to occur. It would be more than folly to decide that the social will be a dinner-dance at a swanky country club when the parish is composed of low-income, socially deprived people. It would hardly lead to the establishment of basic trust and understanding among L and the leadership group (T) so necessary to the forward thrust toward the attainment of the goal. In all areas of religious education the desired outcomes are those which are most appropriate for Christian living. For teachers to relate to each other socially may not be a specific outcome for Christian living, but it may well be a start in the right direction.

The Cove model, in its inclusion of commitment (C_1), consistency (C_2), cooperation (C_3), and communication (C_4) as vital to the climate and to the total effectiveness of a specific project, also sets up a feedback system which is the key to accountability. It is more than that—it is accountability operationalized.

Unless the goal is very narrow, its attainment should provide momentum toward the achievement of other parish goals. For example, creating the spirit of camaraderie among teachers and assisting them to be competent religious educators may be the desired outcome, or G, of a specific process. However, the teachers may then become so concerned about involving parents in the program that they join the pivotal group (T) in a process to achieve this end. Thus, L becomes T and the learners (L) are the parents. It is the dynamic fluidity of the model which makes it effective in all T-L situations. When L join T to form a larger group of concerned adults, commitment (C_1) has been established and is evident to the faith community. Usually a core community is formed which gives a solid base to the parish program. However, it is important to beware of comfortable core groups in which members are so involved in patting themselves and each other on the back that they lose sight of the challenge to formulate a viable religious education program. There must be consistency (C_2) between what the group is doing and what it set up as its goal. It is to this end that accountability is so important, for it provides the group with the opportunity to evaluate all aspects of the goal which together they set for themselves and in the process to revise, or reject, that which they determine ineffective.

Accountability, operating within the framework of shared responsibility, will move beyond this initial stage. The pivotal group must constantly ask itself "What did we set out to do? Are we doing it? If not, why not?" Getting honest answers to these questions requires cooperation (C_3), patience, and time. Eventually, if the group is functioning effectively, it will be challenged through some form of evaluation to demonstrate what it has accomplished. This should be a welcomed experience, because if the group is accomplishing nothing that is all that will be expected of it. It would be well for the group to devise its own criteria against which it will do its own evaluation, so that at some point in time it can render an account of its stewardship to the faith community (C_4).

It is not the intent of this chapter to design an evaluative tool. In fact, whether or not a tool could be or should be designed which is applicable to every parish is debatable. A program should evaluate against the backdrop of the underlying spirit of the faith community, what the parishioners expect of its religious education program, the reasons for having a program, etc., and it is reasonable to assume that this would be different for every parish. However, questions must be asked and answers must be given if the climate for accountability is to prevail.

Basically, before a parish religious education program can be viable and an evaluative tool designed, there needs to be an expressed philosophy of religious education which reflects the attitudes of the parish towards religious education. Certainly, there should be no contradiction between the parish philosophy of religious education and other aspects of parish life. For that reason the philosophy cannot be written by the pivotal group of the program alone. It must be shared and shaped by representatives of other groups in the parish community. However, care should be taken in this process that those involved are not caught up in pretty little phrases which mean absolutely nothing when translated and applied to the living reality of parish life. It would be far more honest to express the conviction that the parish should be financially autonomous and translate that into "we will run a bingo every Tuesday night" than it would to write that the parish will demonstrate deep concern for the socio-economic injustices in the community which is translated "times are tough." The philosophy of the parish, and especially its religious education program should be simple and brief—simple and brief so that opportunities can be provided for all to be intimately acquainted with it. Acquainting teachers and parents with the philosophy provides a splendid opportunity for "housecleaning" namely, evaluating old programs and procedures, adopting new ones. Examining the text in view of the philosophy is often an eye-opener. It may alert teachers to their need for an ongoing educational program and/or teacher development program. Some teachers may even decide that possibly the Baltimore Catechism (1932 ed.) does not have all the answers; that they have not (and possibly cannot) accept the changes in the church and resign from the program. This is healthy. Whether the response is viewed as positive or negative, at least there is action in the faith community, and where there is a "stirring of the waters," there is hope for growth, and growth is a sign of life.

Writing the philosophy of religious education and communicating its meaning to the parish members should also provide the opportunity for acquainting them with the shift in religious education from a child-centered to an adult program. This will necessitate a whole shift in attitudes in most places where the concentration has been on the child, especially as he/she prepares for eucharist, penance and confirmation. An explanation of the philosophy, especially if done in smaller group sessions, may make adults more sensitive to their needs in their relationship to others, to God and to the church. Besides representation from all groups in the parish in arriving at the philosophy for the parish and the religious education program, care should be taken, in fact, it should be insisted upon that all the clergy in the parish be involved, as should anyone who in any professional way is engaged in parish ministry. Even though not directly concerned with religious education, they should share in and be kept apprised of major developments in the program. This type of accountability can be helpful in avoiding duplication of efforts within the parish as well as be a focus for synchronizing ministerial responsibilities. The more that people are involved in and are aware of the religious education program, the more interest, support, and cooperation can be expected.

It would be incongruous to write about accountability in

religious education without including a special concern for adults who are parents. Parents are accountable in a unique way as the primary educators of their children. In an ideal program, teachers would be available to assist parents, to support in carrying out their responsibilities as well as providing students with the opportunity to share their religious values with their peers. Parents have not only the right, but also, and more importantly, the obligation to know the curriculum of the parish program and to continue the teaching of it in the home. If the parish is interested, there are several models for such family religious education programs available, and the design for one should be according to the character of the parish community. Nevertheless, without parental involvement and interest in the religious education of their children, religious education for children makes absolutely no sense. Accountability is not just a word to be tossed about; it is the cornerstone for building a viable faith community. By virtue of their baptism children have the right to expect that their parents will continue to nurture them in the way of the gospel through Christian living. To simply state that parents have the privilege, right, duty, etc., to educate their children often seems inadequate. Parents have the responsibility to educate their children in Christian living, and teachers only share in the parents' ministry. Parents, then, are accountable to share their faith commitment with their children, and the parish is accountable only to assist the parents with their responsibility.

As stated at the beginning of the chapter, accountability is a great word to cover many areas of concern. However, we ask again, "Where does the buck stop?" In the usual parish community the parish board of religious education, or the education commission of the parish council serve as the ultimate agent in accountability. Furthermore, it is important that the board is in harmony with diocesan programs. Each member of the board should be aware of what the other members are doing. The parish board should also provide some way of sharing with interested members of the parish what is going on in religious education. it is also the concern of the parish board to devise ways and means of receiving feedback regarding their program. The president or chairperson of the board should be conversant with all dimensions of the religious education program. If the president or chairperson cannot assume a leadership position and be accountable to the group, then another member of the group should take on the role. It is not essential to have the title to be a leader.

In summary—Accountability: What does it do?

It helps people to realize that they do not operate in a vacuum.

It can be a basic and effective vehicle for communication in the parish.

It can provide a means of ongoing evaluation for the parish program of religious education.

It insures a continuity in a program and not a hit and miss affair.

It engenders interest among parishioners.

It demonstrates the importance of adult education.

Accountability in the context of this chapter is not equated totally to the type of accountability found or talked about in education. In religious education a volunteer will not fret that his/her salary will not be received or increased because of evaluation. Nevertheless, Christian living can be improved through the process of evaluation. Christian tradition has demonstrated that being accountable to another person can be an effective source of growth. However, if religious education programs continue to be for teachers and children, continue to be child-centered, continue to be clergy-controlled, continue to operate out of touch with the people, then there will be no sharing of responsibility, little accountability, and a lifeless program of religious education. In such a climate there is little or no room for growth.

The challenge of accountability calls us to growth in a life-giving situation of health tension. As baptized Christians each one of us is called to grow and to share ourselves with others in the faith community. Accountability is a vehicle for concerned persons to use to evaluate, improve, and invest their talents in a religious education which serves the growth needs of all parish members.

Questions for Discussion

1. Why would accountability rooted in the broader parish community rather than in specific groups, i.e., the CCD board, lead to a more effective religious education program?
2. Many religious educators attest that they have an understood philosophy of religious education. What advantages are there to having a written philosophy of religious education?
3. Why is it of value to have people other than those directly involved in the program be included in writing the philosophy of religious education for the parish community?
4. While the pastor has the ultimate responsibility for the religious education of the parish, it is a responsibility

that must be shared with the faith community. How can active involvement in and commitment of the parishioners lead to an effective program for Christian living outcomes?

5. What are the characteristics you would be most interested in finding in the pivotal person for your religious education program? Why are these characteristics important?

6. Why is it helpful that the overall design of a religious education program include a support system for those who assume leadership roles in the program?

7. Why is it necessary to identify problems and establish their ownership before realistic goals for a parish program can be established?

8. Accountability is built into the Cove model which can be applied to many parish situations. Why does it involve a commitment of time and energies that extend beyond the parameters of the situation itself?

9. A parish which is truly accountable to itself and to its members has no communications problems. Discuss the implications of this statement as it applies to your religious education program.

VI

Teaching For Dying

As has been stressed throughout this book, to communicate the gospel and to develop a Christian worldview effectively these must be taught not simply as content to be understood and appreciated but as a process to be lived. This Christian lifestyle is the lifestyle of a child while one is a child, of an adolescent while adulthood is emerging, and of an adult when adulthood is reached. At each stage there is a religious maturity concomitant with that of the developmental level of the person. This maturity demands an integration of new knowledge and experiences as these occur. Integration occurs subtly and is shaped, as is all learning, by previous experience. As in other areas of learning, integration of knowledge, feelings, and behavioral responses in religious living should not be assumed but needs to be planned for and tested.

Among the most important areas in which awareness increases as one matures is that of the inevitability of death. The acceptance of the finality and inevitability of death is one of the tasks of maturing and, therefore, of developing a mature religious lifestyle. The idea of death is not an easy one for twentieth century man, especially in a society in which the value of science has become institutionalized and, in general, he tries to repress this threat to the pursuit of happiness. Edgar Jackson, who has written extensively on pastoral care subjects, warns that refusing to deal directly and openly with death creates a vacuum of unanswered questions in which anxiety and fear can grow unchecked. Fear of death is more and more being considered the basic fear of man, a fear which can take many forms, such as depression, sundry psychosomatic symptoms, and varying psychological disturbances.[1] Yet, even in religious instruction, the reality of death is often ignored. This silence may partially account for the fact that, despite its clear relationship with death, religion has not been shown empirically to have made any significant difference in the way people face the inevitable.[2]

American society, especially since its emergence from World War II, has experienced a waning of faith in the providential and the sacred. With the increasing pressure of urgent social problems and the growing impersonality emerging from a technologically dominated world, there is an increasing deritualization of grief and mourning which accompany major transitions in life. Mobility has contributed to the decline in the kinship group, separation, divorce, and remarriage to the increasing fragmentation of the family. The lack of a sense of transcending value in life's most encompassing situations has pervaded society. It is most evident in the decreasing respect for life and the increasing denial of death and/or of any transcending significance for death. While the work of Elisabeth Kubler-Ross and Carl Nighswenger[3] has begun to change this picture there remains a wide gap between professed Christianity and the daily living of most Christians.

In conjunction with this cultural denial of death or of its transcending significance there is the constant exposure to violence and threats to life depicted by every form of the mass media. This focus robs death of its feeling while at the same time causes man to be more conscious than ever before of humanity's fragile mortality. Whether these daily confrontations with death are healthy or destructive hinges largely on the various aspects of the educational process. Through graded and continuous efforts, the present social and cultural denial and avoidance of death, particularly in its affective aspects, can be changed. There are many psychological considerations which lead to the realization of the need to come to grips with man's fear and denial of death. The basicness of this fear is certainly one of these considerations. Two other factors which should motivate ongoing death education are the hindrance to emotional growth which denial of death can cause and the importance of one's view of the future in steering present behavior responses.[4]

In light of religion's traditional role of providing the framework for answering questions proposed by death, the integration of death education with religious education seems an especially appropriate way to change current attitudes as well as to insure the completeness of the religious education program. Integrating the inevitability of personal death into one's philosophy of life is an absolute necessity for the development of a Christian lifestyle and worldview. In this regard, Robert Ochs declares that faith which has not come to grips with death is not a tested faith, for death is *the* temptation to faith.[5] Religious education provides the opportunity for this temptation to be introduced and met as an aspect of the process by which one's faith becomes a lived religion.

Like all education, religious education aims to equip the learner to live in a world where men are mortal. However, it also strives to develop lifestyle behaviors which reflect conviction of the gospel message of redemption based on faith in the resurrection. To authentically relate to and live out a resurrection-based faith, one must have learned to accept death without debilitating fear or anxiety. In *Questions and Answers on Death and Dying,* researcher-psychiatrist Kubler-Ross states her belief that preparation for death should start early. She believes that teaching children and young people to face the reality of death would prevent their having to go through all the stages of dying when they are terminally ill and have so little time and energy to deal with unfinished business. Dr. Ross is emphatic in her persuasion that one lives a different quality of life when one has faced one's finiteness.[6]

Certainly religious education, by its facilitation of the formation of a religious worldview, is concerned with quality of life. As Jackson points out, basically all religions have been concerned with building a sound philosophy of life and death to help man cope with his spiritual nature in relation to the physical event we call death.[7] The response to man's yearning for some type of immortality is shaped in each religion by revelation, whether oral or recorded. It may take the form of belief in reincarnation as it does in many Eastern religions, or it may be the conviction of resurrection as it was for the Pharisees and is for Christianity. Whatever the religious response is, it is promulgated and preserved through religious instruction, formal or informal, since it is through the religious education process that worldview and lifestyle are nurtured. It is religious education which promotes the personal discovery of the meaning of life through religious insights. By this means the anxieties about life and fears regarding death can be confronted and new understandings integrated into the maturing personality.

As those who advocate death education point out, the underlying intention of such a program is to help people relate better to reality. The general purpose of formal death education is to engender a greater love of life while reducing the denial and the fear of death. In this way, persons are enabled to develop positive attitudes which help them to respond to death's inevitability without the despair and denial which excessive fear can trigger or without the shallowness of life which denial can allow to develop. Likewise, a developmentally structured religious education is the process of guided confrontation through which the questions of meaning can be faced, deep anxiety about life and death can be resolved, and through which people's lives can be made as productive and as developmental, as creative and as satisfying, as happy and as long as they can be. In this way, as Jackson points out, "the maturing individual can achieve the self-understanding and the self-realization that provide him with a working philosophy of life that is competent to face all there is to life, even its mark of mortality."[8] Upon reflection it is easily seen that the overall aims for death education are congruent with the general aims for religious education. This is of primary importance for Christians as both death education and religious education within Christianity find their beginning point and their conclusion in the mystery of the resurrection: Jesus' resurrection, from which present life takes its meaning and on which its hopes for a new life are built.

The intimate connection between death education and faith in the resurrection is both evident and strong for the Christian. There is, however, for most Christians, many of whom are actively involved in the church's educational endeavors, a rather formidable gap between belief in the resurrection and a theology of death. This deficit is supplied for by the average person in a rather simplistic and frequently unarticulated manner. It usually runs something like: Death is unfortunate but God makes up for it by the promise of a new (and, by implication, better) life. This lack of a developed theology of death makes it even less likely than in other areas of religious education that the coordinator or the individual teacher can assume a uniform theological orientation.

While a uniform theological orientation to the human reality of death is not required, it is necessary that in the Christian community, in general, and among religious educators in particular, there be, with variations, an articulated theology of death which incorporates recent thinking on this matter. When evaluating the climate (as described in Chapter II) in which religiously oriented death education occurs, it is well to be mindful of Jackson's warning that the traditional teaching as it pertains to death may be at variance with the cosmology, psychology, and theology with which today's young people are growing up.[9]

Religious education is not a world unto itself. If the religious community does not reinforce what is taught, it is unrealistic to expect it to be learned in the sense of being lifestyle-producing. Inclusion of the theology of death as well as the related need for death education on all levels on the agendas of in-service programs for religious educators is a step toward filling the need. Only after the initial efforts have been made to educate the educators can one look at the climate of death education. Commitment on the part of the teacher includes an integration of death in a philosophy of life rooted in belief in the resurrection. A teacher sensitive to the group will be able to ascertain the degree of development of a similarly grounded philosophy and can structure the teaching-learning experiences accordingly.

This global view gives stability and consistency to the religious educational process.

Aware of his/her own attitudes toward death, the teacher is free to lead others in their coming to grips with this human reality. While it is true that only a relatively minor role in the development of a Christian worldview and a lifestyle consistent with this outlook is, in fact, given to the formal religious education program, the committed teacher will make the most of all opportunities. Consistency, or harmony, between who the teacher is and what he/she is doing, allows the teacher to do this while encouraging learner input regarding goals, activities, and conclusions reached. Commitment and consistency permit that flexibility which is demanded for lifestyle educational objectives. This is especially true in regard to death education since nonverbal cues can often reveal unconscious anxieties denied in verbal proclamations of attitudes and beliefs. In particular, a teacher must be able to evaluate learner development and openness to further development before attempting to shape attitudes in this often fear-evoking area. Furthermore, as the teacher structures the teaching-learning situation to explore the possibilities of development, the evaluation process continues, providing constant feedback and direction.

This sensitivity to needs and openness must reach beyond the immediate teaching-learning situation into the various segments of the parish and/or the diocese which are concerned with religious education. The idea of explicit death education or even of the more general version of education for loss or grieving is still foreign to many. Aware of society's attitude toward death and, at the same time, conscious of the need for societal reinforcement for effective teaching-learning, anyone wishing to incorporate graded and continuous death education into the religious education program realizes that cooperation with parents, other teachers, and the wider community is an absolute necessity. Programs designed for family religious education suggest themselves as an ideal place to introduce death education. Another possibility is to conduct the death education simultaneously in youth and parent or adult groups somewhat as programs of preparation for eucharist, penance and confirmation are administered today. Finally, it seems that the efficacy of instruction on death and grieving could be greatly enhanced by pulpit preaching designed to complement it.

Following a recent two-week (twenty clock hours) workshop on death and dying, one participant summed up her reactions in the following statement which is quoted with permission:

> "In the midst of life we are in death." Over the past two weeks I have looked at life in death. All that surrounds us is in the process of life in death. Until I was forced to *stop, look,* and *listen* to life in death, I had not given it much thought. My own death and the death of others can be looked at now in a more realistic way. I am not saying I can face death without panic, yet, because of meditation, reading, discussions, talks, speakers, films, I have at least a greater awareness and peace concerning death. The readings, whether they were medical, legal concepts, or a personal history certainly have given me insights that I could never have reached on my own.
>
> As for cognitive learning I have gained much. Areas in dying and grieving that I had never heard of, let alone considered, have been brought to my attention. I believe that I can truthfully say, I can look on death in a more positive way.

My ability to understand a child's view of death and how to help a child come to a realistic view of death is certainly greater. It is still an area that I must meditate and probe. I think it is an area that needs much thought on the part of all. We do a lot of damage to children when it is not handled in the right way."

During the workshop all available means of communication had been utilized in an effort to offer in the two-week session as all-involving an encounter with death and grieving as possible while recognizing the variety of affective states which existed in the group. Though teacher-learner and learner-learner communication sometimes broke down, often due to predetermined response expectations or limitations, the interaction, once restored, was usually on a deeper level and contributed to mutual growth.

Whatever the level of death education, the climate, goals, specific objectives, and structured activities must be mutually reinforcing. The role of the teacher in achieving this delicate balance on the formal educational scene is a major one. However, in regard to death education, as in other areas which have deep though often unacknowledged affective roots, the parental role is very important. The child's rate of development in the understanding and acceptance of death, including the religious dimension, are influenced by parental interpretations of early, personal death-related experiences. This was illustrated by a small scale survey conducted during the aforementioned workshop on death and dying.[10]

Traditional Christian teaching which tends to focus on life before and after death rather than on the process of dying or the need for grieving was very evident in the responses of all the families except one. Interestingly, only one parent voiced awareness that parents by their attitudes toward life, death, and hereafter were teaching their children whether they realized it or not. In each case, the child's ideas about death and afterlife mirrored those of the responding parent or parents as the following four examples illustrate. In citing the responses, the following abbreviations are used: M = male, F = female, P = parent, C = child. Subnumbers indicate family groupings while numbers in parentheses give the child's age.

In the first example the family has the oldest among the children responding. All three youths reflect the mother's inability to talk about death and lack of reference to afterlife.

Question:	How much should be taught to children about death?
FP_1:	Enough to know about.
Question:	How should the concept of death be taught?
FP_1:	I don't know.
Directions:	Write down what comes to your mind about death.
FC_1 (11):	You can die in many ways. (Drawing showed no certain age for death which is caused by illness.)
MC_1 (15):	It's like falling in water where the currents are swift under the water, forcing you under, looking above, seeing the sunlight on top of the water, then seeing nothing drowned DROWNED D R O W N E D .
FC_1 (18):	My opinion about death is that I don't want no one to die, especially my family.

In the second example both parents strongly felt children should know about death's inevitability and finality but are not as strong in their conviction of afterlife. This is reflected in the children's answers and drawings.

Question:	How should the concept of death be taught?
FP$_2$:	With the hope that there is a life after death.
MP$_2$:	By giving a lecture, not by a spanking.
Question:	How do you deal with the concept of death with your own children?
FP$_2$:	I tell them that the person has gone from here and is going to go to Jesus's house.
MP$_2$:	I feel that they will eventually realize that this is life and that one day everyone has to go.
Question:	If your children ever experienced a death, how did you handle it?
MP$_2$:	They have never experienced a death. I hope they never do. We did have to give our pets away when moving. They have cried about it and wished they could see them again, but I feel that would be worse.
Directions:	Write down what comes to your mind about death.
FC$_2$ (7):	When people die you don't see them any- more. You feel bad. People get buried. (Drawing showed dead body off by itself; the face sad and the predominant color black.)
FC$_2$ (9½):	I think death is not very bad because you have a new life and can be with God. (Draw- ing was in two sections. The lower section showed herself, clad in a long pink dress, in her grave. The upper section showed heaven and two unidentified, but winged figures. Below the drawing was written: One day I'll be glad to be with God.)

In the third example the mother's responses showed a hesitancy about telling the child very much and she preferred to focus on religious reasons for death and on the life after death. Even though old enough to have a fairly developed concept of death, the children's answers revealed none.

Question: If your children have experienced death, how did you handle it?

FP_3:   I tried to explain the reason for a person dying, such as the Lord had need for that person, and that he will be very happy and free of suffering.

Directions: Write down what comes to your mind about death.

FC_3 (12):   Going to a new world, heaven.

FC_3 (also 12): The first thing that comes to my mind is that it is the end of the world for me and I will go to heaven with Jesus and it is the beginning of a new world. (Drawings of both girls pictured heaven as clouds marked with crosses and containing single figures.)

In the fourth example, the mother's answers reveal an integrated philosophy of life and death. The parents' efforts at death education are reflected in the children's answers.

Question: How much should children be taught about death?

FP_4:   After age seven children need to have discussion of death. Parents can share their beliefs that God's love is forever, that God will raise us, too, and that Jesus' resurrection is our sign and promise of this.

Question: How should the concept of death be taught?

FP_4:   By honest answers to any questions children

have and through reverence for life. A positive attitude should be nurtured, that life is not taken away merely changed.... We parents do not understand everything about death but cannot withdraw from our responsibility because of our own problems with death.

Question: How do you deal with the concept of death with your own children?

FP$_4$:   ... We also teach that we can experience new life in our struggle to grow, to mature as we become aware of our relationships, how we accept others and how we "die" to ourselves by responding to others.

Directions: Write down what comes to your mind about death. If you cannot write yet, ask Mom or Dad to help you.

MC$_4$ (3):   No answer

FC$_4$ (11):   Death is sad and happy. After life here, you start a whole new life in heaven with God. (Drawing illustrated these two separate lives, one in a coffin, one as a very colorful spirit in heaven.)

FC$_4$ (13):   Death means sadness to me but it is also a time for joy. Death means leaving my life and my friends here but it also means life with God. (In explaining her four level drawing this young lady stated: The contrast of my colors also has a meaning. On earth there is no meaning compared to heaven. The color is black. As you move up, purgatory is brown as waiting. As you enter heaven the colors are of bright and brilliant

lights. You are cleansed by the purity of
white in heaven. You are pure!)

The far reaching effect of an early death-related experience is attested to by the empirical work done in this area
during the past fifteen years.[11] This effect is clearly illustrated in an example cited by one mother in the survey from
which the above quotes were taken.

Question: How do you deal with the concept of death
                 with your own child?

FP$_5$:   When my son at three and a half years of
                 age experienced what death was (two little
                 friends drowned), he was for a long time
                 very afraid of someone dying. He was
                 forever with this constant fear of someone
                 else dying and he would always start to cry
                 when just thinking about it. I sent him to
                 kindergarten. I tried to calm him by saying
                 that death was not the end to life but only
                 the beginning as there is a life after. In a
                 way, I think he still fears death for he fears
                 going too close to water. He wants to take
                 care of me even now.

Directions: Write down what comes to your mind about
                 death. If you cannot write yet, ask Mom or
                 Dad to help you.

MC$_5$ (8):   When someone dies, a part of God dies. I
                 am sorry when someone dies, but there is a
                 new life. (Drawing of "death" showed only
                 the new life aspect. This was illustrated by a
                 simple smiling person with qualities other
                 than human: wings, rays of light, halo, sur-
                 rounded by clouds.)

The foregoing examples were cited chiefly to highlight

parental influence on the development of a child's attitude toward death. This attitude is at first (roughly speaking in children under three) perceptual rather than conceptual. For example, while MC_4 had no verbal response to the meaning of death, he would lie face up on the floor, arms and legs extended, stating "I'm dead," and then rise to continue his play activities. Until about five years old, the child views death as temporary and not necessarily universal. For the five to nine year old and often beyond this age, death is frequently personified, an external agent coming to get one. The final state in the cognitive understanding of death develops over a period of years and recognizes death as final (permanent) and inevitable.[12]

In the responses of parents and children, however, it could be noted that cognitive understanding of death is not automatic with chronological development nor is it equivalent to affective acceptance and integration into one's philosophy of life. Often death understood cognitively is affectively denied. Frequently the religious education of the person has aided this division by placing the emphasis on life after death.

It is possible that theology's renewed interest in the incarnation, in Jesus as true man, will by extension give a clearer focus to death education in our religious educational endeavors. Jesus valued life, but not life over mission. He did not seek death nor hasten it by joining the Zealots nor did He flee death by minimizing his vocation nor by joining the Qumran community of the desert. Jesus believed in a God of the living and hoped for resurrection. Certainly one development of a Christian lifestyle includes the imitation of Jesus' attitude in this behavior shaping dimension of one's worldview.

In our country there has always been a concern that education be related to life. This is equally true in regard to religious education. Education for dying, rooted in the total acceptance of the gospel message, enables the Christian to die for God as well as to live for God.[13] In sound death education instruction, dying and grieving are not minimized but are placed in perspective by our Christian beliefs and the hopes based on these beliefs. Death education gives the learners a chance to verbalize ideas, fears, and uncertainties they have in regard to dying, death, and after-life in a relatively nonthreatening atmosphere. It provides the opportunity for both teacher and learner to integrate more fully a philosophy of life and of death, realizing that, contrary to the common expression, resurrected life is probably not a "whole new life" but rather one whose fullness depends on the growth and maturity achieved in this present life.

Formal death education, especially when it builds on and is supported by informal death education in home and pulpit, provides the time and the space to bring into conscious awareness death and the need for grieving. When this increased consciousness is accompanied and informed by increased understanding of the gospel witness to the resurrection, fear and anxiety regarding death can be reduced.

There are several ways of incorporating death education into one's religious educational efforts. The most obvious is to use occasions as they arise, for example, the death or near death of a pet, a grandparent, or a schoolmate. A newspaper clipping, a story read, or even a chance remark can initiate death instruction if the teacher is attuned to the need for it. A second possibility is to build in occasions for reflection or discussion. Lent, for example, with its emphasis on the suffering and death of Jesus, provides many opportunities for a mini-lesson on suffering, dying, death, and grieving. Other situations can be created with a little imagination and can be very helpful in establishing a climate where death-related topics can be discussed without inhibitions. A favorite is to encourage the learner to imagine him/herself a few weeks prior to birth and that somehow he/she is given the choice of whether to be born. After allowing time for reflection, the teacher initiates the discussion by asking a volunteer for his/her answer with supporting reasons. From the more competent students a panel could present the beliefs of selected religions on any one or more of the following topics: immortality/reincarnation/relation of living to dead/resurrection.[14]

The latter is close to a formal or full-period lesson which, though it takes more time to prepare, usually pays higher dividends in regard to percentage of class involvement, more specific objectives and (though not always) more learning occurring. The following two lessons are offered as guides to structuring a learning experience in death education. While the first is more suitable for the learner under fourteen and the second sample more for the older learner, both can be adapted to almost any group by a teacher who knows his/her group's needs and developmental levels.

Lesson: The Wishing Well

Behavioral Objectives[15]

Discusses his fear of death without shame. (A2)
Relates the universality of death and the universality of redemption. (C3)

Teacher Notes

Behind every fear there is a wish. Quite possibly behind or beneath the fear of death is the ego's wish for immortality. The lesson is structured so that there will occur the opportunity to deal with this connection and, in doing so, possibly to surface the often suppressed fear of death and to examine some of its roots. It is especially important to affirm that man's fear of death is natural and in no way something to be ashamed of and is, in fact, often mitigated through an open discussion. In this way the learner can be led to see that fear can be positive, e.g., preventing individual or mass suicide or negative, e.g., preventing one from doing anything that is difficult or challenging.

Product-content and Process-content

On the preceding day tell learners that tomorrow we shall talk about wishes. Instruct them to think about what they would wish for if they were permitted ONE wish. Ask for volunteers to construct a wishing well or wish box for tomorrow's lesson.

On the day of the lesson try to structure a setting where a wishing well would likely to be found. (Put the chairs aside or in a circle, sit on the floor, if possible, or go outside.) Put the wishing well in the center. Pass out pieces of paper on which each one, including the teacher, can print his ONE wish and drop it into the wishing well. Each then pulls a wish, reads it aloud, and offers his opinion on (1) the *possibility* of its being fulfilled and (2) the *value* of the wish considering each had only one wish. Wishes should not be judged good or bad but only (1) the possibility of its fulfillment and (2) of its relative value. The teacher should be very conscious of every opportunity to lead the students to a realization that some wishes are not possible without God's help and that many of the deepest wishes of man, such as peace, overcoming death, and achieving lasting happiness are promised to us in Christ.

Lesson: Suicide: A Solution?

Behavioral Objectives

Differentiates between Jesus' death for us and suicide. (C2)
Shows regard for life by refraining from taking and making dares which involve high accident or death risks. (A5)
Resolves never to judge a person who commits suicide. (A5)

Teacher Notes

The general goals of the lesson are (1) to assist in the discovery that suicide can be a result of the fear of death (as an attempt "to get it before it gets me") or of a wish for death, (2) to sharpen these mental processes which aid in the distinction between an inevitable death which is given value and a suicide, (3) to put the seemingly good aspects of suicide into proper balance, (4) to deepen the understanding of why Christianity has always frowned on suicide, and (5) to show how the bereaved of a suicide often need more support and comfort than those bereaved in other ways. The last mentioned is a basis for the church's recent change to a more human position on the funeral and burial rites for one who commits suicide.

Debate should be geared to the learners' previous experience in this area. The simplest is to have each side present its views, each speaker being given three to five minutes. Then allow time for the members of each side to confer and choose one person to rebut the chief arguments of the other side. After this, the discussion could be opened to the group *for points not already made.* Allow a few minutes of reflection before asking that once again learners choose to sit on the side that expresses their view the most closely.

Product-content and Process-content

Before the lesson have the learners list all the possible arguments for one side (whichever they prefer) of the proposition: Suicide is (is not) a good means of solving one's problems.

On the day of the lesson select a few representatives for each side. Ask the remaining learners to sit in the half of the room designated to correspond to their position at the moment. Tell them that at the conclusion they will make this choice again.

In conclusion draw on the board a see-saw, putting "regard for life" on one end and "suicide" on the other to illustrate the notion that the probability of suicide is directly related to one's regard for life. Ask the learners what resolutions for their own lives should come from today's look at suicide. The teacher should have in mind those of importance which may be overlooked. In passing one could mention the recurrence of this resolution-type thinking in popular songs, for example, the country hit "Take time to touch some morning" (before it slips away). One could also mention clubs which try to make the most of life and life's possibilities, e.g., 4H Club, Scouts, etc. One with which some may not be familiar is MAKE TODAY COUNT, an informal organization of terminally ill patients which emphasizes appreciating everything, every moment for as long as they have. Their motto is: "Look to the stars and the sun for your tomorrows, for as many as you will have of them."

The above lessons can also be used as a foundation for building a unit in death education suited to the present theological orientation of you and your students. In this area as in all others of religious education, the learner must remain primary with product-content and process-content working harmoniously to achieve lifestyle objectives.

There are few events in the human experience that trigger so much fear and anxiety and are so consistently avoided as dying and grieving. Yet, paradoxically, there is nothing in life so inevitable. If our religious education efforts do not touch this area with the liberating message of redemption, freeing the learner to meet the challenge of discipleship wholeheartedly, it fails, whatever else it accomplishes. That this freedom from fear is a real need, even among our children, is illustrated by the following poem written by fourth graders during a recent poetry workshop. The topic for the composition was not assigned and the poem is quoted with the permission of Carol Massar, the conductor of the workshop.

It's a shriek of cold air!
It's paralyzed—like you're full of lead and can't move
                    like something's sticking to you and
                    you can't get away
Your throat is dry
You're all weezy inside
Your heart's going to crack open
Needles are being stuck all over in you
And you want to get in a safe little corner
        get in the car with your Mom
Scared, you see, is
        Thinking somebody's next to you when nobody's
        around
        Imagining somebody in the window when you're in
        bed
            at night
        Dialing 226-3232 and hearing a scream [Note:
        Number is for correct time]
        Never being able to go to sleep, ever.
When you're scared you shiver in a freezing rain
AND YOU'RE AFRAID TO DIE
AND YOU THINK, IT'S MY OWN LIFE. I ONLY HAVE
ONE LIFE!

Questions for Discussion

1. What effort have you made to integrate a philosophy of death into your philosophy of life?

2. At what age does one become aware of and accept the inevitability of death?

3. What is the relationship of religious education and death education?

4. Peter Koestenbaum suggests that fear of death may be the primal fear from which all others stem. Has your experience lead you to agree or disagree with his analysis?

5. How would you approach death education with a group of seven year olds? seventeen year olds? a seventy plus group?

6. How can Ochs call death *the* temptation to faith?

7. What are some of the ways in which man-as-man shows his longing for immortality?

8. How would you respond to parents who object to their children having death education because it is morbid?

9. How is it possible that death education could increase rather than decrease the fear of death?

10. What are some of the reasons formal death education should be encouraged?

VII

The Prophetic Role of Religious Education

Not too many years ago one feature of the preached mission, stirring enough to bring the borderline impenitent attender to a firm resolution of improvement, was the meditation on death in the presence of the draped catafalque. This was prophetic in its intent, in its symbolism, and often in its effect.

Current criticisms from many corners regarding today's religious educational programs as being too-far-left, or too-far-right, or too-middle-of-the-road may be the catalyst needed to stir religious educationalists to bring their endeavors to a prophetic level. Only when religious education is prophetic on the parish, diocesan, and church levels can it hope to affect the wider society which Marshall McLuhan so aptly called the global village. To speak of being prophetic is to imply the new, the not-yet, the pull of the future and to do so somehow challenges the present. The challenge carries a summons and often elicits from those addressed both the attraction and the repulsion that reference to change usually produces: the excitement and yet the threat of thinking beyond the at-least-it-is familiar present condition. Those involved in religious education frequently are aware that presently it is not as effective as it could be and that it seldom reaches the prophetic level. Yet there is often the unnamed and undefined desire that the efforts expended in religious education should be and could be reaping more far reaching and longer lasting results. This concern could be described as the desire that religious education be prophetic in its intent, in its characteristics and in its effects. However, before elaboration on the prophetic role in religious education can proceed, there must be some discussion, first, of prophets and prophetic role and, secondly, of the conditions which facilitate the accomplishment of the prophetic goal.

As John O'Grady remarked, a bit sarcastically, at the beginning of the decade, "Prophets these days are on the rise. . . . Every aspect of society is infected."[1] Still the question remains: What is a prophet? Unfortunately, in the course of time, the prophet has become one who foretells the future. Literally and biblically the meaning of prophet is different. Here he/she is one who speaks out on behalf of someone else. The Hebrew prophet is sent by God to declare God's word or God's will to the people. By speaking for God, the prophet proclaims judgment and promise, revealing men's sins to them that men may recognize them, repent, and be forgiven. The prophet is commissioned to bring the people to a deeper knowledge of self and of God's merciful presence in their lives despite their sins. Behind the prophet's sting is love and compassion. As Abraham Heschel states, "The prophet is not only a censurer and accuser but also a defender and consoler. . . . In the presence of God he takes the part of the people. In the presence of the people he takes the part of God."[2]

In the context of preaching of sin and judgment, the prophet would sometimes refer to the future, indicating the awful consequences of lives divorced from the moral will of the Lord. These references to the future were most often by way of warning. They were threats graphically expressed in hopes of engendering repentance that even if it did not eliminate the need for punishment for sins already committed, it could deter future transgressions or insure faithfulness through the time of misery. At other times, however, the prophet might speak of future in terms of the good things to come, foretelling the redemptive action of God and assuring the people of the marvelous things God had prepared for his faithful ones. Though highly descriptive these pictures of the future, whether heartening or disheartening, are outbursts of poetic translation of the basic principle that evil is its own undoing. Sin is seen as affecting the entire life of man: biological, social, political, economic. Evil is seen as the corruption of all that is good and if left unchecked would reduce the world to its primitive chaos. The prophets viewed the religious corruption of the people as the source of all evil.[3] Hence they could not be silent. When, therefore, they spoke of the future it was only from emotions generated by the people's disregard of the moral will of the Lord, not in the popular notion of the prophet's being a high-class fortune teller. The principal concern of the prophets was the current situation, the events that challenged their lives and the lives of their contemporaries. Any reference to the future was always in relation to and flowing from the events contemporaneous to themselves and their listeners.

The prophets were of the nature of extraordinary preachers, men who dramatized by word and action the meaning of total commitment to the moral will of the Lord. Often a crisis precipitated the coming of the prophet, but always he/she addressed issues of fundamental religious importance. Jeremiah in the Hebrew scriptures and Jesus in the gospel accounts provide two of the most obvious examples of prophetic word and action.[4] Jeremiah, for example, is told

> You shall not take a wife nor shall you have sons or daughters in this place. For thus says the Lord concerning the sons and daughters who are born in this place, and concerning the mothers who bore them and the fathers who begot them in the land: "They shall die of deadly diseases. They shall not be lamented nor shall they be buried; they shall be as dung on the surface of the ground" (16:2–4a).

This is certainly a prophetic action in a culture which views offspring as one of the chief forms of immortality.

The potter provided Jeremiah with an analogy for some of his most powerful prophecies. At one time he says:

> ... I went down to the potter's house, and there he was working at his wheel. And the vessel he was making of clay was spoiled in the potter's hand, and he re-worked it into another vessel. ... Then the word of the Lord came to me: "O house of Israel, can I not do with you as this potter has done, says the Lord. ... If at any time I declare concerning a nation or a kingdom, that I will pluck up and break down and destroy it, and if that nation ... turns from its evil, I will repent of the evil that I intended to do to it. ... Thus says the Lord, behold I am shaping evil against you and devising a plan against you. Return, every one from his evil way, and amend your ways and your doings" (18:1–12).

Elsewhere he combines prophetic word and action, being directed by the Lord to

> "Go, buy a potter's earthen flask, and take some of the elders of the people and some of the senior priests and ... proclaim ... 'Thus says the Lord of hosts, the

God of Israel, behold, I am bringing such evil upon this place that the ears of everyone who hears of it will tingle. Because the people have forsaken me . . . I will make void the plans of Judah and Jerusalem, and will cause their people to fall by the sword before their enemies, and by the hands of those who seek their life.' . . . Then you shall break the flask in the sight of the men who go with you and shall say to them, Thus says the Lord of Hosts: So will I break this people and this city" (19:1–4, 7, 10–11).

Despite his efforts to relate the word of the Lord to the lives of his people, Jeremiah, at least in the short run, felt none of the satisfaction of a job well done.

This is a familiar story to all who have read and meditated on the gospel accounts with their many examples of Jesus' prophetic words and actions. Encouraging to most Christians are the parables of forgiveness, for example, that of the Prodigal Son (Lk 15) and of Lazarus and the Rich Man (Lk 16). Likewise, Jesus' parables of the kingdom offer the hearer assurances both that the kingdom is ultimately the work of God and that God is slow to anger and rich in mercy. The first is seen, for example, in the parable of the surprising harvest, harvested rather complacently.

The kingdom of God is as if a man should scatter seed upon the ground and should sleep and rise night and day, and the seed should sprout and grow, he knows not how. . . . But when the grain is ripe, at once he puts in the sickle because the harvest is ripe (Mk 4:26–27, 29).

The long-suffering of God toward his people preached so convincingly by Hosea, Jeremiah, and other prophets is illustrated by Jesus in the parable of the grain and the weeds:

> The kingdom of heaven may be compared to a man who sowed good seed in his field; but while men were sleeping, his enemy came and sowed weeds among the wheat. . . . So when the plants came up and bore grain, then the weeds appeared also. When his servants inquired if they should gather up the weeds, the master replies, "No, lest in gathering the weeds you root up the wheat along with them. Let both grow until the harvest" (Mt 13:24–26, 29).

Like Jeremiah, Jesus strove to convey his message by prophetic action as when he chose the Twelve (Mt 10:1–4) or when seeing Levi the son of Alphaeus sitting at the tax office he said to him, "Follow me" (Mk 2:13–14). Probably the most dramatic combining of prophetic word and action, apart from the passion narrative, occurred when

> The Passover of the Jews was at hand, and Jesus went up to Jerusalem. In the Temple he found those who were selling oxen and sheep and pigeons, and the money-changers at their business. And making a whip of cords, he drove them all, with the sheep and oxen, out of the Temple; and he poured out the coins of the money-changers and overturned their tables. And he told those who sold the pigeons, "Take these things away; you shall not make my Father's house a house of trade" (Jn 2:13–16).

Jesus, Jeremiah, and the other prophets were conscious that they were speaking in the name of the Lord. Once they accepted the call they seldom doubted their mission no matter how seemingly uncomprehending those who heard the message seemed to be. Often the prophets' inspiration wasn't recognized as being from God and, for the most part, at least in the short run, their words fell on deaf ears and hard hearts. The prophetic message had to stand the test of time and the prophetic cause had its ups and downs but, in the long run, the prophets succeeded because Israel has never totally succumbed to idolatry.

In many instances the prophet was a traditionalist, being deeply rooted in the Mosaic tradition and being dependent, in both doctrine and language, on the preachers who went before him/her. Yet the same prophet was often, from a different perspective, an iconoclast, challenging the apparently holy and the revered. Beliefs cherished as certainties and institutions endowed with supreme sanctity are exposed as mere scandalous pretensions.[5] Both stances are truly prophetic as both are concerned with the lives of God's people witnessing to their call to be holy because the Lord their God was holy (Lev 19:2). It is this rather extraordinary balance in the teaching of the prophets, despite their profound experience of being called to prophesy, that has given the prophetic utterances their lasting value. The prophets were able to identify with a God who was angered by sin but was merciful to the penitent. They crusaded for a commitment rooted in tradition yet alive to the contemporary situation. They dealt not only with laws and principles but also, perhaps chiefly, with the relations between God and mankind.

The prophet by presence as much as by preaching creates or renews the call to discipleship which brings nascent faith to a living faith. Through word and deed the prophet seeks to give new direction to the community. This is the prophetic mission and any means that are in keeping with this goal and which will facilitate its accomplishment are used.

The prophets were not social reformers. They have no explicit program of political or economic reform. The prophetic perspective is most often, in fact, foreign to economic considerations. Indeed they resemble the revolutionary in that they envision a new order and announce the inevitable destruction of the existing order. However, they have no program for its accomplishment for it is the Lord who brings about both the destruction of the old and the inauguration of the new in His own time.[6]

Using this survey of the work of the biblical prophet, the intent that motivated it, the means which were used, and the effect it produced, one can further delineate the idea of prophetic role, the assumptions which underlie it and its manifestations in the lives of those who are called to practice it, in particular the religious educator.

The practice of the prophetic role virtually eliminates self-seeking since it implies speaking on behalf of another. In the first place this other is God. However, in just as real a sense, the other is the church, the parish community and the family in whose name the religious educator carries on his/her mission. It is this conviction of teaching in the name of the other that aids the religious educator to speak strongly and to maintain consciousness of his/her role, despite the sometimes dispirited reaction of the hearers.

To practice the prophetic role is to show a great sensitivity to sin. This sense of the corrupting influence of evil leads one to expose it in order that the sinner might repent of his ways. To achieve this the religious educator strives to bring the learners to a deeper knowledge of self and of God's redeeming presence in the church and in their lives. In all of his/her religious instruction, the religious educator maintains this dual announcement of sin and of mercy. He/she is vitally concerned with the relationship of God and consistently strives to develop in the learner a living faith which nourishes a mature religious lifestyle within a Christian worldview.

The prophetic role is aimed at far-reaching and long-lasting results. In all things it keeps in focus that the chief goal of all religious education is that God's people witness in their lives the call to be holy as their God is holy. Of the prophet, Heschel says that he proclaims the highest good is to practice kindness, justice, and righteousness.[7] Like the prophet the religious educator hopes for success in the short run also but often only achieves long-run success in regard to the general goal. Lifestyles are created slowly. Hence, while it is legitimate and advisable to plan for and look for achievement of specific objectives, these particular successes must not be allowed to substitute for the ongoing work of facilitating a Christian worldview and lifestyle behavior patterns.

This is not to imply that religious educational endeavors are essentially future oriented. This, in fact, would be unprophetic. As was seen, the prophets were primarily concerned with the current situation and with the lifestyles of their contemporaries. Present behavior was measured against their call and previous evidences of God's love for them. References to the future were always outgrowths of the contemporary scene and summoned changes which would produce a future different from the present, one in which God's kingdom would come. Likewise, the religious educator is working within the present situation, in lives that are being lived right now. All work is limited by the maturity level of the group as well as by the degree of religious maturity of the religious educator. Yet within the striving to improve the present there is always the pull of what-could-be. It is in maintaining this tension that the religious education program plays a prophetic role.

This challenge to the present is both exciting and scary. On the one hand it prevents nostalgic thinking that past glories will carry one through present times. On the other hand it attempts to give new direction to the community. It opposes the euphoria of those who think that nothing has changed and who are mollified by unprophetic voices which sanctify the status quo. At the same time it preserves its traditional roots, keeping God and his moral will as primary. As the prophets opposed the tendency to treat any institution or phase as if it were definitive,[8] so the religious educator must be alert to the likelihood of over institutionalization or of institutional stagnation, even of the possibility of being a contributor to it. With this balance between tradition and change, the religious educator can take a stand against authority when it is clearly seen that authority is corrupting the tradition either by its prevention of needed change or by its precipitous rush to bring in the new and the different.

The execution of the prophetic role demands that one witness by personal lifestyle as well as by teaching. One who witnesses to the truth of the message by his/her own life lives the message in a way that points to the future for the learners. To do this one must be continually growing and integrating experiences, realizing that no one has ever had all the data of reality. The prophetic religious educator is one who is, in today's argot, a lifelong learner, one always open to the ongoing revelation of God.

In the operationalization of the prophetic role a variety of means is used to facilitate the accomplishment of the overall goal as well as the performance objectives. This often includes the task of raising the community's awareness of the need for change. To carry out the task of religious education effectively, the teacher combines the prophetic word and action, illustrating the desired learning with parables based on examples or analogies familiar to the learner. He/she employs all the means found by educational and psychological research to be fruitful in motivating learning and insuring retention.

For a religious educational program to truly achieve its prophetic role demands time. Lifestyle behaviors and worldview are not built in a few months. Neither are they achieved by a single teacher or by religious instruction limited to sacramental preparation. Only over time and with increasing religious maturity can the learner be led to realize that the kingdom of which Jesus speaks so invitingly is God's kingdom and that man's role, as important as it may be, is to cooperate with the will of God. It takes time to learn to pray "*Thy* kingdom come; *Thy* will be done."

Religious educators like the prophets are not social reformers nor revolutionaries. They are sensitive to evil, to the daily occurrences of injustice in the world. They do feel fiercely. As Heschel puts it: "Prophecy is the voice that God has lent to the silent agony, a voice to the plundered poor, to the profaned riches of the world."[9] As did the prophet so the religious educator envisions a new order in which justice and peace will reign even if this vision can only truly be accomplished with the resurrection. Religious education is not prophetic in that it has a plan to improve the world but rather in that it has hope that in Christ the present order can be redeemed.

What are the conditions which facilitate the effectiveness of the prophetic role? For religious education endeavors to achieve the prophetic it is essential that the parish and/or diocese accepts on principle the possibility of prophetism and that the fear of irreligion (heresy) is not stronger than the openness to change.[10] The prophetic voice is more likely to flourish where the value systems are weak and/or pluriform. Too rigid a faith system stultifies the idea of ongoing revelation which is necessary for prophetism. A healthy respect for differing theological orientations can provide the climate for prophetic religious education.

Certainly it is important that the climate in which religious education occurs be prophetic. It is also essential that those in charge of the program be prophetic in their orientation. They must be willing to denounce sin while lovingly leading the sinner to repentance and a deepened hope in the resurrection. They must be convinced that God is involved in the life of man and therefore must restrain the tendency to totally rationalize away the anthropomorphic language of the bible. Furthermore they need to be persons firmly in touch with the contemporary scene and with the community in whose name they are carrying out their task. Yet they cannot be so submerged in the present order that they are unable to exercise the function of critic. They need to be willing to face established authority when it is clear that such authority is stifling the growth of mature religious living. Above all they must not be self-seeking. Being aware of their assumptions they must be willing to alter any plan when there is sufficient feedback to indicate that the desired long-range goal and/or the performance objectives are not being achieved.

While it is necessary that the climate in which the religious instruction occurs be prophetic and that those chiefly responsible for the religious education be prophetic in orientation, these will not insure that the religious education of a parish and/or diocese is playing a prophetic role. The program itself must likewise be prophetic in its intent and its characteristics. Essentially a religious education program is prophetic in its intent when it remains clearly committed to the general goal of making more explicit a Christian worldview and developing a lifestyle consistent with it.

What characterizes a prophetic religious education program? While there is no infallible guide, some or all of the following features will be found when religious education endeavors are striving to play a prophetic role in today's church and in society. First, the attitude toward religious educators will be prophetic in that there will be genuine concern regarding the appropriate preparation of both teachers and administrators[11] and also regarding the methodologies employed in the instructional process.

While all receive in baptism and confirmation the call to spread the faith indirectly by the witness of one's life and directly though informally when the occasion arises, there is the more specialized call to participate directly in the formal religious education program of a parish or a diocese. It is this latter group which is referred to in the first draft of the National Catechetical Directory which states that all who participate in the catechetical ministry of the word need certain qualities including educational preparation.[12] This directive delineates a hierarchy of needs in which the need for administrators and teachers becomes secondary to the need for *qualified* administrators and teachers. A prophetic religious education program will respect these priorities, declining to schedule religious instruction unless satisfied that the qualities, inlcuding sound and updated theological and educational preparation, are present in those who are to carry out the program.

A prophetic religious education program will be as concerned with how the instruction is given as it is with the qualifications of those who give it. The distinction between indoctrination and instruction will be carefully guarded as will that between cognitive knowledge about religion and religious education. The program will seek to lead the learner to a deeper understanding of the Gospel and to the free choice of gospel lifestyle. To do this the program will integrate educational theory and practice, being regularly guided by clearly stated performance objectives rather than time filling or purely enjoyment producing gimmicks. Such a program will reflect an integration of product-content and process-content with the focus on process-content,[13] which by careful monitoring is prevented from interfering with the product-content. The role of the religious educator will be one more of posing questions than of teaching answers thus aiding people to live open to change within their basic commitment. In this way the religious education experience is simultaneously an experience in Christian living; the teaching-learning experience becomes the prophetic parable. Long-term success is more likely as the learner grows to understand the message of the gospel and to conclude that he/she wants to live that gospel. With this conviction the Christian can then take seriously his/her responsibility to be an effective agent for ongoing growth within the community.

Secondly, prophetic religious education recognizes that formation is a continuing process, always in need of improvement "because of the increasing maturity of the human person and the unfolding of problems."[14] Hence the religious education program is neither child-centered nor adult-centered but rather is learner-centered, providing for all segments of the Christian community on both the parish and the diocesan level. At one time it may be the middle-aged who needs to be encouraged to understand and accept the changes in a church to whose changelessness they have been so loyal. At other times it may be the young adult who suddenly finds him/herself alienated from a church changing too slowly. Then there are always the converts who have special needs and the young learners whose spiritual journeys have just begun. Just as the learners differ so, a prophetic religious educational outlook will initiate differences in the approach, in the specific objectives and in the degree of responsibility the learner is expected to assume for the direction and the success of the endeavors. Like life itself, prophetic religious education is multidimensional and varied, leaving room for the uniqueness of each person while consistently providing for the tie-in of the gospel message, life experience and faith response. As the Vatican II Declaration on Christian Education encourages, a prophetic religious education strives for integration of Christian education into the whole pattern of human life in all its aspects. Thus, for example, values education is conducted within a religious perspective grounded in sound and updated theology.

Thirdly, for religious education to play a prophetic role it must have a community dimension, not only in the sense of striving to include all segments as discussed above but also in that it has an historical perspective and a wide accountability base. This community dimension is an important one on both points. Unless religious educators know where the church has been they cannot be much of a help in its continued growth. An historical perspective permits today's Christians to live out of the past without being bound to it, and to reap the benefits of countless dedicated lives.

Moreover, this sense of community encourages a wider support for all religious education efforts, especially those directed to the young learner. When a religious educator works closely with family and parochial expectations progress is more likely and probably longer lasting since reinforcement has a wider base. In the same manner, the more the spirit of accountability for the content, the process and the effectiveness of the religious education program permeates the parish community, the greater will be the probability of the program's being prophetic. Accountability, discussed in detail in Chapter V, is a consideration in any serious human endeavor. The degree to which religious education is prophetic in a given parish or diocese is most probably in direct proportion to the seriousness with which the community concerned views its accountability for the endeavor.

Fourthly, a relgious education program plays a prophetic role when it balances its recognition that there are many ways of being religious with its concern that for each person religion be both personal and social. This is often the stumbling block in religious educationalists. Primarily the difficulty lies in human limitations. It takes prophetic insight to help people discover religion as a function of their own lives and their own experiences without yielding to the temptation to impose ones own way of being religious. The facilitation of religious experience in others and the highlighting of the social dimension without defining its specific manifestation characterize a truly prophetic approach to religious education. As *To Teach as Jesus Did* reminds us: "To discern the practical demands of justice is often difficult. Yet Christians *must be prepared to perform these difficult tasks of discernment.*"[15]

Only recently has there been in religious education any extended use of the tools of social science. While widespread usage is limited to program designers and publishers, it is beginning to make its appearance in teacher training programs and in instructional settings. In some quarters the application of scientific methodology to religious education is viewed with apprehension. Sometimes the reason for this fear is vague, but it can most often trace its roots to reluctance to change. The use of a social science approach to religious education implies more than a surface change. It is based on a different way of looking at life, a way which is open-ended as well as experience-based and verified. There is, for example, rather convincing evidence that the small group is an important instrument for changing behavior. To accept this finding would seem to demand changes in the scheduling of most teacher training sessions and instructional programs. Yet the principle is often accepted although the required changes of policy do not follow.

To take a second example: Much is said today about the decline of the extended family and the resulting anomie suffered by adults of various ages. The conducting of adult religious education programs, such as single, young, parent, or elderly, could open avenues of growth hitherto untapped. A religious education program based on research findings in education, psychology, sociology, and anthropology is prophetic in using these findings to improve present religious instruction and to conduct experimental programs for future direction. A religious educational program open to the findings of social science research combines free inquiry and empiricism with the existing conceptualizations of world order. It is thus more likely to foster lifestyle behaviors which transcend the present at least in the yearning for the ideal. In this way the religious education program plays the prophetic role by generating within the community witness to the kingdom.

This fifth characteristic of a prophetic religious education program leads to a sixth feature: the ability to generate hope by fostering a Christian worldview in an increasingly non-Christian and often hopeless world. This need for hope grows daily as "coming face to face with our increasing capacity to destroy ourselves and our world has led many . . . to give up not just on one man, or one group of men, but on man himself."[16]

A prophetic religious education enables the learner to

develop a philosophy of life which is marred neither by Nietzschean optimism of the Superman nor by Kalfkan-like pessimism. Such an education is prophetic in that the maturing religious personality becomes increasingly aware that liberation in Jesus encourages the cultivation of good human relations, especially the art of living fraternally with others,[17] and includes the freedom to be happy and to seek satisfaction without guilt. Within such a perspective the Christian understands that accepting God's superiority does not have to emphasize one's own inferiority, especially if God is perceived as being within each person, but suggests that "one of the reasons Jesus Christ is seen as Savior is because he shows that God can be found completely expressed within a person."[18]

This ability to be human religiously, rooted in the hope of the resurrection, is characterized by an increasing conviction that all profound theology and all dimensions of the human condition are mutually pertinent. Deepened appreciation of the interrelatedness of theology and life frees one to value each stage of life as it comes and encourages one to face the inevitability of dying and of human grieving. Religious education in a society as death-fearing as twentieth century United States is certainly playing a prophetic role when by its inclusion of regular death education it facilitates the accomplishment of what 1974 Pulitzer Prize winner and thanatologist Ernest Becker calls the greatest single task of human beings: facing the inevitability of death. When a religious education does this it achieves one crucial measure of success of the educational ministry as outlined in *To Teach as Jesus Did:* "It enables men to hear the message of hope contained in the gospel" (par. 8).

Seventhly, religious educational endeavors are prophetic when there is a clear ecumenical dimension. Teachers and learners should be stimulated to learn more about various religious persuasions so that they may understand the spiritual and moral motivations of others. Speaking at a recent national conference on religion and the teaching of human relations, Martin E. Marty of the University of Chicago reminded his hearers that neither religious commitment nor religious pluralism is going to disappear.[19] Therefore it is necessary that all who are serious about their own religious values understand the faith which directs the lives of their neighbors, whether this faith is expressed in a Western religion or in a less familiar Eastern religion. In an ever shrinking world it is increasingly important that faith be taught without prejudice. Fear that religious commitment would be diminished by nurturing the ecumenical spirit has been the chief deterrent to the inclusion of any meaningful study of comparative religion in most religious educational programs. However, the more prophetic approach realizes that willingness to examine the reasons for separate traditions can deepen religious commitment "since it leads to a humility and openness before the mystery of human lives and our own relationship with God."[20]

To insure an ecumenical dimension in current Christian religious education four areas require systematic attention. The first is the removal of all negative teaching about the other religions from textbooks and other instructional aids or the refusal to use materials which reflect a prejudiced viewpoint. Secondly, and more importantly, as educational methods change and less emphasis is placed on packaged programs, it is vital that those responsible for the religious education endeavors be trained to understand the nature of pluralism and how to teach accurately about other groups while remaining faithful to one's own doctrinal commitments. Thirdly, it is important in building a sense of the oneness of the human family that religious educators include in the curriculum opportunities for the learner to confront global community issues such as hunger, war, peace, racial, or religious prejudices. Finally, it is imperative that one's own tradition be taught accurately. In Catholic religious instruction, for example, it is very necessary that the teaching about Mary be in keeping with that of Vatican II. Taking direction from the Dogmatic Constitution on the Church (Ch VIII), the religious educator will present Mary as one to be venerated as a model of faith and obedience and as a sign of sure hope in the resurrection. Care to guarantee the ecumenical dimension of one's religious education program insures not only its being prophetic but also that it is denominationally more sound.

Lastly, a religious educational program plays a prophetic role in present day United States when, recognizing declining church authority (secularization) and increasing American civil religion (allegiance to the nation as the new Promised Land), it attempts to alter this trend by providing a religious formation in tune with the American approach to life. To do this, the instruction must be in response to a concrete situation. It must be clear that religion's answer can and does make a difference to those who believe it. And, perhaps most importantly, the instruction must occur within a community that supports what is taught by the witness of its lives.[21]

One cannot say what will make religious education prophetic in the future except in the general sense that it will always aim for the total commitment of each individual within the Christian community to the gospel message. In all ages there must be a willingness to use all legitimate means and alternate models to actualize the liberation of Christ for the people of the time. Everywhere prophetic religious education must function as a unifying force in the community,[22] working out of a tradition which is upheld, even in the face of an authority structure that is, however unwittingly, stifling it. Prophetic religious education facilitates an openness to change and growth while it aids in the development of a Christian worldview and lifestyle. True prophetic religious education is tested as is everything in life: by its intent, by its characteristics and chiefly by its effects. It does not just happen, but it is achievable.

Questions for Discussion

1. What are the chief characteristics of the biblical prophet?
2. Why does John L. McKenzie decline to classify the prophet as a social reformer or a revolutionary?
3. Is being a prophet equal to (a) being dramatic? (b) being antiinstitutional? (c) being anxious for recognition for a job well done?
4. What is the relationship of the goal of religious education and the aim of the prophet?
5. How is it possible for the religious educator to be prophetic? In what sense is being a religious educator a mission?
6. In some areas the failure of religious education is attributed to a defeatist attitude on the part of religious educators. Is this true in your situation? How is such an attitude antiprophetic?
7. How are prophetic word and prophetic action part of the teaching-learning process?
8. In evaluating your present religious education program, what signs do you find of its being prophetic?

Epilogue

It has been the intention of this book to emphasize the importance of teaching for Christian living outcomes. The authors have presented an approach to religious education which is specifically directed to those who bear the responsibility for the parish religious education program. The authors introduced a practical working model not only for the weekly teaching-learning experience but, also, for other aspects of parish life. They have provided a brief description of a successful teacher development program which should prove helpful to directors/coordinators in planning long-range goals for their parish programs. The inclusion of the chapter entitled "Teaching for Dying" emphasizes the underlying theme of the book, that is, unless product-content and process-content are similated as Christian living outcomes so that they can be practiced as Christian life-style behaviors, one might reasonably question whether teaching-learning has taken place. It is the reality of our living and our dying as members of the faith community which gives credence to the teaching-learning ministry.

While the book was written specifically with the non-professional teacher in mind, the authors recognize the need for ongoing research and prophetic vision in religious education. It was written to meet a critical need in the present. Research and vision will certainly lead to new approaches and models for teaching-learning to meet the ever changing needs of the faith community. It is a dynamic of growth that needs change and much research should be done not only to determine how effectively we are meeting present needs but also to project possible models to meet the needs of the future church. In response to felt and/or projected needs new approaches have already been initiated in some areas, for example, family religious education, programs for the elderly, for youth, adult concerns, and others. Whether or not these programs are teaching-learning experiences can only be determined by effective, consistent, and ongoing evaluation.

Another major thrust of the book has been an emphasis on the need for all members of the parish to be directly concerned or indirectly involved in the religious education of the total parish. The closing of parochial schools and the rather alarming statistics of the Greeley-Rossi studies certainly indicate that there is a pressing need for creative planning and implementation of programs to meet the needs of a rapidly changing church. It would seem that we can no longer afford the luxury of placidly accepting a program that is geared to and attended by a small percentage of the children in the parish. Just as the schools in the immigrant church met the needs of the Catholic population of its day, so new and creative models which encompass all segments of the faith community must meet the needs of the church in the future. For too long we have centered our attention and energies on the child and neglected other segments of the parish whose needs in many instances were greater than those of the child. It is to be hoped that continuing research, prophetic vision, and the faith commitment of concerned adults will provide the leaven for a major breakthrough and new horizons in the field of religious education[23]

Notes for Chapter II: Teaching for Learning

1. John L. McKenzie, *Dictionary of the Bible* (New York: Macmillan Publishing Co., 1965), p. 870.

2. Walter M. Abbott, ed., *The Documents of Vatican II* (New York: Herder and Herder, 1966), pp. 269–270.

3. *General Catechetical Directory* (Washington: United States Catholic Conference, 1971), p. 84.

4. James Michael Lee, *The Flow of Religious Instruction* (Notre Dame, In: Religious Education Press, 1973), p. 234.

5. Alvin Toffler, *Learning For Tomorrow* (New York: Vintage Books, 1974), p. 14.

6. B. Othanel Smith, "Toward A Theory of Teaching," in *Theory and Research In Teaching*, ed., Bellock (New York: Teachers College Press, 1963), p. 4.

7. W. James Popham and Eva L. Baker, *Systematic Instruction* (Englewood Cliffs, New Jersey: Prentice-Hall, Inc., 1970), p. 17.

8. Lee, *The Flow of Religious Instruction,* p. 235.

9. Ibid, p. 235.

10. Morton T. Kelsey, *Encounter With God* (Minneapolis: Bethany Fellowship, 1972), p. 225.

11. Thomas B. Gregory, *Encounters With Teaching* (Englewood Cliffs, New Jersey: Prentice-Hall, 1972), p. 83.

12. Ibid., p. 88.

Notes for Chapter III: Teacher Development: An In-Service Program for Teachers

1. Norman E. Gronlund, *Stating Behavioral Objectives for Classroom Instruction* (New York: Macmillan, 1970).

2. Mary K. Cove and Rosemarie Mamuska, "Teacher Development Program, Phase I", Diocese of Springfield (Mass.), March, 1976.

3. David Krathwohl, Benjamin S. Bloom, and Betram B. Maccia, *Taxonomy of Educational Objectives. Handbook I: Affective Domain* (New York: McKay, 1964).

4. Cove and Mamuska, "Teacher Development Program."

5. Erik H. Erikson, *Childhood and Society,* 2d ed. (New York: Norton, 1964), and *Identity, Youth and Crisis* (New York: Norton, 1968).

6. Jean Piaget, *The Child and Reality,* trans. Arnold Rosin. (New York: Viking, 1974).

7. Ronald Goldman, *Religious Thinking from Childhood to Adolescence* (London: Routledge and Kegan Paul, 1964), and *Readiness for Religion* (London: Routledge and Kegan Paul, 1965). Further research studies in this area are contained in David Elkind, "The Development of Religious Understanding in Children and Adolescents," in Merton P. Strommen, editor, *Research on Religious Development* (New York: Hawthorn, 1971), pp. 655–685.

Notes for Chapter IV: Theological Dimension of Religious Education

1. Declaration on Christian Education (1965) paragraph 4, reads in part: "Such instruction gives clarity and vigor to faith, nourishes a life lived according to the Spirit of Christ, leads to a knowing and active participation in the liturgical mystery."

2. Reported in Jeffrey K. Hadden, *The Gathering Storm in the Churches* (New York: Doubleday, 1969).

3. For a careful analysis of the influence of theological stance on religious educational practice see Harold William Burgess, *An Invitation to Religious Education,* and Ian P. Knox, *Above or Within? The Supernatural in Religious Education.* Both are published by Religous Education Press, Mishawaka, Ind.

4. James Michael Lee, *The Shape of Religious Instruction,* (Notre Dame, In: Religious Education Press, 1971), p. 11.

5. Gregory Baum, "Responses to Charles Davis," *Studies in Religion* 4 (1975):223.

6. See, for example: Mt 9:13, 18:21–22, and Luke's three parables of God's mercy in Ch. 15.

7. In particular to Peter who had betrayed him and to James and John who were concerned with getting choice places in the kingdom.

Notes for Chapter V: Accountability

1. Leon M. Lessinger, "Principal And Accountability," *Education Digest* 37(1972): 8–10.

Notes for Chapter VI: Teaching for Dying

1. Herman Pfeifel, "Attitudes Toward Death: A Psychological Perspective," *Journal of Consulting and Clinical Psychology* 33 (1969):294–95.

2. David Lester, "Experimental and Correlational Studies of the Fear of Death," *Psychological Bulletin* 72 (January, 1967):27–36: Glen M. Vernon, *Sociology of Death* (New York: Ronald Press, 1970), p. 203.

3. The works of Kubler-Ross are frequently cited both in this chapter and in most material on death and death education. Due to his early and untimely death, the contributions of Nighswonger are less well known. The cassette study program, featuring Nighswonger and produced by Creative Resources, Waco, Texas, is an invaluable aid for anyone interested in this area, especially for those in any form of Christian ministry.

4. Feifel, "Attitudes Toward Death," p. 293.

5. Robert Ochs, *The Death in Every Now,*" (New York: Sheed and Ward, 1969), p. 15.

6. Elisabeth Kubler-Ross, *Questions and Answers on Death and Dying* (New York: Macmillan, 1974), p. 4.

7. Edgar N. Jackson, "Suspended Death," in *Religion and Bereavement,* ed. Austin H. Kutscher and Lillian G. Kutscher (New York: Health Sciences Publishing Corp., 1972), pp. 97–98.

8. Edgar N. Jackson, "The Theological, Psychological and Philosophical Dimensions of Death in Protestantism," in *Explaining Death to Children,* ed. Earl A. Grollman (Boston: Beacon Press, 1967), p. 194.

9. Ibid., p. 180.

10. Eight Catholic families attending the Pastoral Institute but not enrolled in the Death and Dying Workshop were contacted by Angela Persano, S.H.F. and Katherine Erdahl, S.H.F. Seven parents and eleven children responded on prepared forms. The results are quoted with permission.

11. See, for example, Herbert C. Archibald, "Bereavement in Childhood and Adult Psychiatric Disturbances." *Psychosomatic Medicine* 24 (1962): 343–351; Albert Cain and Mary Erickson, "Children's Disturbed Reactions to the Death of a Sibling," *American Journal of Orthopsychiatry* 34 (1964): 741–752; G. M. Levinson, "The Pet and the Child's Bereavement," *Mental Hygiene* 54 (1967): 197–200.

12. Based primarily on the pioneering work of Maria Nagy and on subsequent studies by psychologists and educators.

13. Randolph Crump Miller, *Live Until You Die* (Philadelphia: United Church Press, 1973) expresses interestingly the relation of dying to living: a Christian who gives his living to God continues to do so in his dying, by accepting death so that God's work can be carried on by those who are still healthy.

14. In the October, 1975 issue of *Religion Teacher's Journal,* Sr. Theophane Power offers a very interesting approach to death education for the intermediate grade youngsters.

15. Objectives are classified as cognitive (C) or affective (A)

according to Bloom and Krathwahl's taxonomies described in Chapter III and the level is indicated by the arabic number.

Notes for Chapter VII: The Prophetic Role of Religious Education

1. John F. O'Grady, "A Question of Prophets," *American Ecclesiastical Review* 162 (June 1970): 392.

2. Abraham J. Heschel, *The Prophets* (New York: Harper & Row, 1962), p. 24.

3. John L. McKenzie, *The Two-Edged Sword* (Garden City, New York: Doubleday Image Books, 1966), pp. 181, 183–84, 185.

4. Quotations from the text of the bible come from Herbert G. May and Bruce M. Metzger, eds., *The Oxford Annotation Bible with Apocrypha*, Revised Standard Version (New York: Oxford University Press, 1965.)

5. Heschel, *The Prophets*, p. 10.

6. McKenzie, *The Two Edged Sword*, pp. 190–91.

7. Heschel, *The Prophets*, p. 9.

8. Roger Aubert, ed., "Prophets in the Church," *Concilium* 37 (1968):2.

9. Heschel, *The Prophets*, p. 5.

10. Based on the article on Prophets in *Sacramentum Mundi*, ed. Karl Rahner, Vol. 5, pp. 110–113.

11. For a more detailed discussion see Alfred McBride, "Preparing Teachers and Administrators for the Field of Religious Education," *Horizons* 3 (Spring, 1976): 59–64.

12. National Conference of Catholic Bishops Regional Meetings, *National Catechetical Directory*, Third Draft, Spring 1977, ch. VII, Part A, Sec. 174.

13. Stanley Keleman, *Living Your Dying* (New York: Random House, 1974), p. 115, notes a similar need for therapists. He says

that in workshops he has to remind participants over and over to focus on process, forget product in order to deepen the process of living.

14. "Decree on the Apostolate of the Laity," art. 29, par. 6, in William M. Abbott, S.J., ed., *The Documents of Vatican II* (New York: Guild Press, 1966).

15. National Conference of Catholic Bishops, November 1972, *To Teach as Jesus Did,* paragraph 11, emphasis added.

16. William Gaylin, "Caring Makes the Difference," *Psychology Today* 10 (August, 1976): 38–39.

17. "On the Apostolate of the Laity," art. 29, par. 5.

18. Stoudenmire, John, "The Role of Religion in the Depressed Housewife," *Journal of Religion and Health* 15 (No. 1, 1976):66.

19. Sponsored by the American Jewish Committee and St. Louis University, Fordyce House, St. Louis, Mo., June 1975.

20. Thomas E. Kramer, Representative for Religious Education of the United States Catholic Conference at the Conference footnoted above.

21. Based on Patrick C. Rooney, "Religious Instruction in the Context of Catholic Schooling," *Notre Dame Journal of Education* 3 (Fall, 1974):270–274.

22. Dennis McCarthy, "Prophet and Community," *The Way* 11 (1971):67–68.

23. For a further discussion of the prophetic role of religious education see James Michael Lee, ed., *The Religious Education We Need,* (Mishawaka, Ind.: Religious Education Press, 1977), especially the final chapter written by the editor.

Index

academic study of religion,
approaches to, 4
accountability
an effective source of growth,
123-24
characteristics of, 110-13
stewardship, 110-11
celebration, 111-12
listening, 112, 113
enterpreneur, 112-13
community obligation, 163-64,
171
Cove model and, 100
parish religious education and,
99, 102-5, 109-10, 117
through in-service education,
54
American society since WWII, 26,
127, 166, 168

behavioral goals
activities and, 69-70
current textbooks and, 64
course content and, 11
description of, 10-12
guides for selecting, 62-4
how to state
for the affective domain, 61-2
for the cognitive domain,
58-60
value of, 57-8

communication
nonverbal, 44, 48
verbal, 44

death
affective acceptance of, 140-1
cognitive understanding of, 140
developmental attitude toward,
139-140
theology of, 140
death education
as anxiety reducing, 128-9, 141
lifestyle objectives and, 146
need for, 128-30, 166
parental role in, 134-40
religious education and,
128-30, 146
suggested means to accomplish,
141-2
sample lessons, 142-6

faith
death and, 128
development of, 62
measurement of, 15
religious education and, 15, 156
without prejudice, 167-8

habits, 20-1

teaching for living, 7–8, 21–2, 29,
    31, 73, 126, 162, 168, 170
teaching-learning situation
    affective dimension
        reemphasized, 6, 45
    affective impediments to, 46, 85
    communication skills and, 46–9
        listening, 47–8, 56, 85
        questioning, 47
        responding, 48
        storytelling, 49
    previous experience and, 84
    testing success of, 75–6, 81
teaching models, 30–1, 36–8
    Cove model, 30, 38–46, 50, 71,
        78
        climate, 39–41, 55, 63–5,
            141–2, 160
        commitment, 41–2, 86, 100,
            132
        communication, 43–4, 102–3,
            132
        consistency, 42, 100–1, 132
        creating an effective religious
            education program and,
            117–9

Lee model, 37–8
Popham and Baker model,
    36–38
teaching theory
    basic criteria for, 35–6
    teaching models and, 36
theology
    behavioral goals and, 92–3
    doctrine and, 90
    influencing product-content
        and process-content, 82–4,
        89
    in-service education and, 86–7
    need for updating in, 163
    of death and resurrection, 140
    of death needed, 131
    range of theological orientations,
        84–5
    religious living and, 90
    ritual and, 90
    Scripture and, 90

value education, 6, 17–8, 26, 163

worldview, 7–8, 12, 128–9